Poems From Eastern England

Edited by Claire Tupholme & Michelle Afford

YoungWriters
First published in Great Britain in 2007 by:
Young Writers
Remus House
Coltsfoot Drive
Peterborough
PE2 9JX
Telephone: 01733 890066
Website: www.youngwriters.co.uk

SB ISBN 978-1 84602 913 4

Foreword

Young Writers was established in 1991 and has been passionately devoted to the promotion of reading and writing in children and young adults ever since. The quest continues today. Young Writers remains as committed to the nurturing of poetic and literary talent as ever.

This year's Young Writers competition has proven as vibrant and dynamic as ever and we are delighted to present a showcase of the best poetry from across the UK and in some cases overseas. Each poem has been selected from a wealth of *Little Laureates* entries before ultimately being published in this, our sixteenth primary school poetry series.

Once again, we have been supremely impressed by the overall quality of the entries we have received. The imagination, energy and creativity which has gone into each young writer's entry made choosing the poems a challenging and often difficult but ultimately hugely rewarding task - the general high standard of the work submitted ensured this opportunity to bring their poetry to a larger appreciative audience.

We sincerely hope you are pleased with this final collection and that you will enjoy *Little Laureates Poems From Eastern England* for many years to come.

Contents

James Ashford (10) 1

Barrington Primary School, Barrington

Adam Day (10) 2
Cameron Douglas (11) 3
Tom Lee (10) 4
Daniel Rule (11) 5
Joshua Taylor (11) 6
Kate Woodland (10) 7
Emilie Alard (11) 8
Ben Cattley (10) 9
Emily Iggulden (11) 10
Matthew Davis (10) 11
Tommy Froggatt (11) 12

Bicker Preparatory School, Bicker

Luke Grimer (10) 13
Isobel Gibbs (9) 14
Lydia Tunnard (11) 15
Katie Worrall (11) 16
Georgia Higgins (11) 17
Lewis Higgins (8) 18
Charlotte Houldershaw (8) 19
William Wallace (7) 20
Edward Cooke (8) 21
Harvey Wild (7) 22
Charlotte Hill (7) 23
Saskia Smith (8) 24
Vienna German (8) 25
Jordan Kingswood (9) 26
Lauren Stanley (7) 27

Earl of Dysart Primary School, Grantham

Shai Clarke (8) 28
Ebony Pacey (9) 30
Joanne Larsen (9) 31
James Cronin (8) 32
Naomi Prentice Martin (8) 33
Lilly Newhouse (8) 34

Aiste Stankeviciute (9) 35
Helen McLardy (9) 36
Fae Blake (8) 37
Nathan Smith (8) 38
Jorge Goncalves (9) 39
Kyarna Priest (8) 40
Grayson Barnes (9) 41
Jodie Finney (8) 42
Ellie-Mae Brown (8) 43
Rhiann Moir (8) 44
Leah McGhee (9) 45

Great Doddington Primary School, Wellingborough
Honor Drummond (10) 46
Kirby Carter (11) 47
Sean Sinfield (10) 48
Matthew Parsons (10) 49
Lauren Wood (10) 50
Elliott McLester (11) 51
Molly Underwood (11) 52
Lawrence Jefferies (10) 53
Amarn Rowe (10) 54
Jack Greenacre (11) 55
John Davies (10) 56
Jodie Summers (10) 57
Oliver Chatterton (10) 58

High Ash CE Combined School, Great Brickhill
Brad Baines (10) 59
Lucy Billington (10) 60
Savannah Mercer (9) 61
Harriet Mahier (9) 62
Stephanie Boad (9) 63
Owen Rickard (10) 64
Alexander Ford (10) 65
Barnaby Collins (9) 66
Olly Margrave (9) 67
Jay Bowdler (9) 68
Bradley Watts (9) 69
James Blaesbjerg (10) 70
Abigail West (10) 71

Robert Valledy (10) 72
Antonia Leech (9) 73
Anna Irwin (9) 74
Danny Burke (9) 75
Harry Renson (10) 76
Fraser McGrath (9) 77
Samuel Hardwicke (9) 78
Megan Searle (10) 79
Ryan Watts (9) 80
Emily Whittall (9) 81
Hollie Canham (9) 82
Harry Strong (9) 83

Holtspur School, Beaconsfield
Cameron Arkley (6) 84
Matthew Smout (9) 85
Laurren Bowler (8) 86
Kelsie Elliott (9) 87
Chloe Rees Pearman (8) 88
Sarah Clark (9) 89
Alistair Beard (9) 90
Billy Cochrane (9) 91
Matthew Foster (9) 92
Aiya Flatman (8) 93
Connor Jackson (9) 94
Owen Galera (8) 95
Lulu Pratt (9) 96

Molescroft Primary School, Beverley
Holly Tucker (9) 97

Park Junior School, Wellingborough
Trent Woodley (8) 98

Putteridge Junior School, Luton
Amy Gardner (11) 99
Shannon Williams (10) 100
Sian Shannon-Sinclair (11) 101
Lara Burton (10) 102
Amy Pollard (11) 103

Kiera Hobbs (10) 104
Ben Evans (10) 105
Lucy Jefferies (11) 106
Mark Waterhouse (10) 107
Jack Dinsey (10) 108
Ellie Hudson (10) 109
Kyle Grizzell (10) 110
Ellie Chittenden (9) 111
Sebastian Cooper (10) 112
Sophie Risbridger (10) 113
Ibara Razaq (10) 114
Harkirit Rayatt (9) 115
Alex Coles (10) 116
Bethany Freeman (10) 117
Stephen Osborne (10) 118
Joe Perry (11) 119

Ranskill Primary School, Retford
Kim Fleming (11) 120
Rachael Wilkinson (10) 121
David Gough (10) 122
Abigail McMahon (9) 123
Mary MacDonald (9) 124
Sam Johnson (9) 125
Daniel Brownson (8) 126
Hannah Richardson (9) 127
Jill Fleming (8) 128
Kesson Wyld (8) 129
Ryan Alder (9) 130
Caitlin Bennett (8) 131

Rollesby First School & Nursery, Rollesby
Sophie Windsor (8) 132
Loretta Askew (8) 133
Maria Jacobs (7) 134
Annabel Thain (7) 135
Millie Hewkin (8) 136
Jasmine Williams (7) 137
Anthony Abel (7) 138
Alice Austin (8) 139

St Thomas More Catholic Primary School, Leicester

David Kyei-Mensah (9) 140
Isabella Oreffo (9) 141
Edward Ellis (9) 142
Katy Cooper (10) 143
Demi Boyce (9) 144
Clare Ruane (9) 145
Daisy Connolly (10) 146
Imogen Howell (9) 147
Isabella Ambrico (10) 148
Eleanor Pierson (10) 149
Daniel O'Dwyer (9) 150
James McErlean (10) 151
Lisa Konomoore (8) 152
Joe Muddimer (8) 153
Ameerah Dawood (9) 154
Shannon Sheffield (8) 155
Kobe Whiteman (9) 156
Niamh McErlean (8) 157
Rose Leather (8) 158
Max Lewis-Clarke (9) 159
Molly O'Halloran (10) 160
Tobit Dehnen (9) 161

The Fairway First School, Norwich

Harris Tzokas (7) 162
Jonathan Reynolds (7) 163
Alice Walker (7) 164
Fin Smith (8) 165
Mia Morgan (7) 166
Milo Butler (8) 167
Jaideep Chopra (7) 168
Alex Wong (8) 169
Charlie Grisley (8) 170
Eamon Hatoum (8) 171
Irene Ashworth (7) 172
Alex Law (7) 173
Billy Breame (7) 174
Haroon Said (7) 175
Shreya Arya (7) 176

Josh Bunn (7) 177
Chloe Cox (8) 178
Linton Garrod (8) 179
Caleb Coxhead (8) 180
Louis Hall (7) 181
Sophie Bloomfield (7) 182
Olivia Finch (7) 183

Waulud Primary School, Luton
Abbie Cochrane (10) 184
Billie Hardiman (11) 185

Wellow House School, Newark
Iaomie Malik (10) 186
Mary McQuilkin (11) 187
Harriett Hawkins (11) 188
Will Langley (11) 189
Matt Badcock (11) 190
Charles McQuilkin (10) 191
Rive Malik (9) 192
William Cundy (9) 193
Chloe Lidgett (10) 194
Zoe Buckland (10) 195
Sam Lawrence (10) 196
Jack Whitfield (10) 197
Troy Booth (10) 198
Grace Brown (9) 199
Aiden O'Beirne (10) 200
Lizzie Lee (8) 201
Ed Radley (11) 202
Charles Broughton (11) 203
Rosie Radley (10) 204

Woods Loke Primary School, Oulton Broad
Aaron Homes (8) 205
Chloe Tiborez (8) 206
Isobelle Read (8) 207
Eleanor Sanders (9) 208
Frances Lear (9) 209
Joshua Butcher (9) 210

Charlie Church (9) 211
Hannah Heath (9) 212
Rebecca Thomas (8) 213
Bethany Paisley (8) 214

The Poems

Summer Holiday

Animals are going in the sun
They think it is fun

People running about
When they go out

Children climbing trees
They get the breeze

In the swimming pool
Then you are cool

Hot as the sun
It will cook a bun.

James Ashford (10)

The Park

The trees fishing while the sun is awakening
The pond silently watches the people go by
The fence standing tall and strong and proud
The path waiting for people to walk on it.

Adam Day (10)
Barrington Primary School, Barrington

My Dog Is A . . .

Finger biter
Shoe chewer
Dog pooer
Mischievous face
Food stealer
Sharp claws
Face licker
Stick fetcher
Ball chaser
Food gulper
Fast runner
Silky coat
Bright brown eyes
Wet black nose
Tail wagger
Red collar
Mites, ticks and fleas
This is my black Labrador . . .
. . . Ruby Crinkle Douglas.

Cameron Douglas (11)
Barrington Primary School, Barrington

The Motorway

One sunny day the sun was rising
The fog was drifting from the road
The road still sleeping in a flash
The moving cars shot past.

The road awakened with a fright
Trees swayed from side to side
The barn concealed from the noise
Hiding in the greenery.

The sign standing proudly
On the side of the road
The barrier feeling the wind
From the cars' speed.

As the day came to an end
The cars began to vanish
In the distance the road
Went to sleep calmly.

Tom Lee (10)
Barrington Primary School, Barrington

A Man Called Fin

There once was a man called Fin
Who got cut on a pineapple tin
He squealed like a pig
On the floor fell his wig
Now he wished he hadn't bothered with puddin'!

Daniel Rule (11)
Barrington Primary School, Barrington

The Silver Path

It starts at a white scene
On the banks of Lake Hycene
A path so silvery grey
So all the people say
It leads up to the waterfall.

The sky so black and grey
Reaches to the mountain's bay
All the trees whisper in dismay,
'He's here, he's here today!
The great river god,' they say.

He was there all and all like a tank
His head lifted out of the riverbank
As the trees stirred
Another sound was heard
The sound of the clouds weeping.

'The gale is coming! The gale is coming!
All you creatures go a-runnin'.'
The gale passed over the riverbank
A tree fell into the river and sank
But at last the wind sighed
And made way for day.

Joshua Taylor (11)
Barrington Primary School, Barrington

Kate Is . . .

Kate Louisa,
Teacher teaser,
Trainer wearcr,
Never swearer!
Lesson-time chatterer,
Does it matter?
Late arriver,
Blames the driver!
Netball player,
Ponytail swayer,
Sports leader,
Fluent book reader,
Arsenal supporter,
Perfect daughter.
Kate!

Kate Woodland (10)
Barrington Primary School, Barrington

The Wind - Cinquain

Blowing
Trees bending down
Whipping at my cold cheeks
A disruptive meditation
Damaged?

Emilie Alard (11)
Barrington Primary School, Barrington

Fire - Cinquain

Fire, fire,
Warming and bright
Liquid, solid or gas?
Blazes of colourful danger
Friend, foe?

Ben Cattley (10)
Barrington Primary School, Barrington

The Sun - Cinquain

Burning
Heating the Earth
Gleaming down from Heaven
Unmistakable rays of light
Shining.

Emily Iggulden (11)
Barrington Primary School, Barrington

Old Man Jock

There once was a man called Jock,
He thought he had a pet rock,
People guffawed,
Some even roared,
When Jock noticed his rock was a sock!

Matthew Davis (10)
Barrington Primary School, Barrington

Young Frog

There was a young frog from Glasgow
Who was chased by a big fat hippo
When the hippo went mad
The frog leapt from his pad
And landed in the soft snow.

Tommy Froggatt (11)
Barrington Primary School, Barrington

Love

Love is like a big red heart.
Love sounds like the birds tweeting in the trees.
Love smells like a brand new perfume.
Love looks like flowers blossoming in the breeze.
Love feels like excitement at Christmas time.
Love tastes like Dairy Milk chocolate melting in your mouth.
Love reminds me of when I went to Lanzarote in the swimming pool.

Luke Grimer (10)
Bicker Preparatory School, Bicker

The Alien Invader

I am an alien invader,
Do not be alarmed,
I come in peace,
You never shall be harmed.

I come in search of help,
My planet is at war,
Do not be afraid,
Hop in and close the door.

Almost there,
Here we are,
Be very careful,
I will shut the door.

Thank you for your help,
Here is your reward,
Use it very wisely,
It's a trip to Mars!

Isobel Gibbs (9)
Bicker Preparatory School, Bicker

Lydia's Mother's Day Poem

To me you're always kind,
You always wash and clean,
You scrub and scrub and scrub and scrub,
Until things are to gleam.

You'll always be my friend,
I love you very much.
You always make me feel safe,
When it's me you touch.

My mum works very hard,
I'm extremely glad to say;
Thank you for all you do,
Happy Mother's Day.

I hope you love me too,
You're very, very fun.
I love you lots and lots and lots,
You'll always be my mum.

Lydia Tunnard (11)
Bicker Preparatory School, Bicker

I Want . . .

I want to go to Saturn,
Jupiter and Pluto too.
I want to go to Mars
I want to see the stars.

I want to go to the moon,
To see if it's made of cheese.
I want to have no gravity,
I'll fly to space with ease.

Katie Worrall (11)
Bicker Preparatory School, Bicker

My Mum

My mum is fun,
She'll say kind and thoughtful things
And that is my mum.

She'll cook my favourite:-
Honey roasted parsnips and carrots
My mum likes Sudoku very much
And that is my mum.

She does lots of thoughtful things,
Through lots of different ways
And I love my mummy lots and lots,
And that is my mum.

She does the best brown sugared meringues
I think they're very yummy
I think she does the best fruit cake
And that . . .
Is . . .
My . . .
Mummy!

Georgia Higgins (11)
Bicker Preparatory School, Bicker

Football Crazy

Every time I try to play football
I ask my brother to join me
He always says no
I feel so much woe,
'Please, please, please,' I say,
'No, no, no, no,' he'll say.

Lewis Higgins (8)
Bicker Preparatory School, Bicker

The Magical Horse

On a fine day
Hear the magical horse
On her way
Getting closer and closer
Then galloping away
Over the hills she goes
Soaring high up in the air
And back down again.

Charlotte Houldershaw (8)
Bicker Preparatory School, Bicker

The Moon

At night I can see the moon shine brightly
In my eyes and spooky cats around
The trees at night when I go to sleep
I hear *bang, bang*
And then I see the moon disappear
Then it turns dark and the moon
Comes back again.

William Wallace (7)
Bicker Preparatory School, Bicker

Mustard And Custard

Mustard and custard in a pot
Mustard and custard nice and hot
Mustard and custard eat the lot
Mustard and custard well I'm not!

Edward Cooke (8)
Bicker Preparatory School, Bicker

Darkness

I'm afraid of the dark
I think of ghosts in the dark
The moon shines through my
Bedroom window in the dark
Dark is when Santa comes.

Harvey Wild (7)
Bicker Preparatory School, Bicker

My Birthday

At my birthday I get
Lots of presents,
The best bit I like is
When I get the cake,
I like to get lots of
Chocolate cakes,
I was seven in 2006.

Charlotte Hill (7)
Bicker Preparatory School, Bicker

The Rainbow

The rainbow has seven colours,
Just seven, that is all.
If there were six colours,
The rainbow wouldn't be a rainbow at all.

Saskia Smith (8)
Bicker Preparatory School, Bicker

My Mummy

My mummy is very nice,
She gives me lots of love,
My mummy is the best,
The best in the world.
If I could I would,
Give her my heart.
She is the best in the world.

Vienna German (8)
Bicker Preparatory School, Bicker

A Stormy Night

A stormy night, the wind wails,
A stormy night, the thunder bangs,
A stormy night, the lightning strikes,
A stormy night, the doors bang,
A stormy night, the windows smack against the wall,
A stormy night, the curtains dance,
A stormy night, I am cold!

Jordan Kingswood (9)
Bicker Preparatory School, Bicker

My Mum

My mum is kind to me,
My mum cooks me cookies,
My mum looks after me when I am poorly,
My mum takes me out for dinner,
My mum plays with me.

My mum.

Lauren Stanley (7)
Bicker Preparatory School, Bicker

Colours Of The Rainbow

Red
Rubies are shiny, sparkly and beautiful to wear.
Roses have a wonderful scent and are beautiful for Valentine's Day.
Cherries are sweet, lovely and juicy to eat.
Apples are shiny, delicious and sweet to eat.
Blood is runny, dribbling and very unpleasant.

Yellow
The sun is hot, bright and very delightful.
Sunflowers bright, gentle petals waving in the wind.
Canaries are bright yellow and feathery, flapping their wings in the
gentle breeze.

Pink
Pigs snuffing and snorting, rolling in mud.
Flamingos are soft, emotional and very tall like a giraffe's neck.
Lipstick is light pink, soft and smooth like fur.
Eyeshadow is dark pink and smooth like a river of pink chocolate.

Green
A crocodile is dark green, has bumpy scales, very mean and can
strike at any time.
Watch out!
Emeralds are sparkly, worn on a queen's finger
Grass is wavy, rustly and good like a trampoline that kids
like to play on.

Purple
Amethysts are shimmering and sparkling, worn on a queen's crown,
as purple as a Pegasus horn.
A wizard cloak is bright purple, twinkling in the night like a moon
sparkling.
Poison bubbling and spitting when you drink,
it's the end of your world.

Orange
Fire's flames frightening you. Fire bulging out of a house. *Run!*
Sunsets are wonderful, beautiful and lovely to sit and watch.
So relaxing.
A goldfish's scaly, shiny like a crocodile's scales on his back.

Blue
Sapphires are shiny, glimmering like the ocean at sunset.
Dolphins are jumpy, playful and cool to swim with like you're on
Free Willy's back.
Skies are light blue, twinkling like a sapphire shining in the night sky.

Shai Clarke (8)
Earl of Dysart Primary School, Grantham

The Colours Of The Rainbow

Red
Cherry - juicy, delicious taste to eat.
Ruby - a ruby on the queen's finger with joy
Rose - a red rose, beautiful, as red as a strawberry.

Yellow
The sun - yellow as it sparkles with delight in the blue sky
Sunflower - swirling and twirling as it grows it grows in the
green grass.
Canary - the canary flying with delight as it gets blown into a tree.

Pink
Pig - pink pig as pink as one can be
Flamingo - a flamingo walking on the path pecking for food
Lipstick - I put my lipstick on nearly every day but it goes away.

Green
Grasshopper - the grasshopper jumps and bumps
Crocodile - the crocodile swam as fast as it could but stopped to go
munch, munch!
Grass - the green, green grass waving around in the bush.

Purple
Amethyst - the jewel sparkling within the queen's laboratory
Wizard's cloak - the wizard's cloak made into ice cream
Potion - the purple potion made into a bubbly drink.

Orange
Fire - the flame in the fire was making more flames
Sunset - the sunset in the sky was orange like fire
Goldfish - they're pretty and so, so fast.

Blue
Dolphin - the dolphins are so cute and big
Ocean - the ocean is blue, as blue as a bluebell
Sky - the sky is blue and the sea is too.

Ebony Pacey (9)
Earl of Dysart Primary School, Grantham

The Colours Of The Rainbow

Red
A rose, clear, beautiful, smells sweet.
The ruby is a dark precious stone like on the Queen's crown.

Pink
Pig, it has a curly tail
Lipgloss makes your lips look fabulous.

Green
A crocodile has lots of different shades of green; as well as
sharp teeth.
Grass, it can be wild or it can be normal grass.

Purple
Potion can make you shrink as small as a mouse
Amethyst - a purple precious stone.

Orange
Fire - lots of flames which come from a dragon's mouth.

Blue
Ocean, very wavy, beautiful, calm and very still.

Joanne Larsen (9)
Earl of Dysart Primary School, Grantham

The Colours Of The Rainbow

Red
A ruby is a very pretty gem, especially when it is in red,
Blood comes out a human's soul,
Cherries are very tasty and delicious.

Yellow
The sun is even hotter than lava, that makes it the hottest thing
in the universe,
Sunflowers are the prettiest plant in the country,
A canary is a very pretty bird.

Pink
A flamingo is very beautiful,
Pigs are fat and very pink,
Pink T-shirts are very cool.

Green
Grass - is a very common habitat,
Alligators are green and scary,
Emeralds are the biggest jewel in the world.

Purple
Perfume smells very nice
Jewels are very nice.

Orange
Oranges are very tasty,
The sunset is very beautiful,
Goldfish is a lovely sea creature.

Blue
The ocean is a very tropical place,
The sky is beautiful,
Sharks may act evil but inside they aren't.

James Cronin (8)
Earl of Dysart Primary School, Grantham

The Colours Of The Rainbow

Red
Cherries are small, soft and tasty to eat,
Strawberries are nice and red rosy,
Roses are red, as red as blood.

Yellow
The sun is so yellow and bright,
Sunflowers are as yellow as dandelions.

Pink
Pigs are as pink as their tails,
Flamingos are as pink as their feet,
Lipstick is as pink as the colour pink.

Green
Crocodiles are as green as a canal,
Grass is as green as the stem of a flower,
Emeralds are as green as grass,
Lizards are as green as a crocodile.

Purple
A wizard's cloak is purple with stars and moons.

Orange
Oranges are so sweet and sour,
Starfish are orange and spotty.

Blue
Dolphins are as blue as the ocean,
Blueberries are like the ocean.

Gold
Rings are as gold as the sun,
Necklaces are as gold as rings,
Bracelets are as gold as necklaces.

Silver
Zips are as silver as plugs,
Plugs are as silver as irons,
Irons are as silver as zips.

Naomi Prentice Martin (8)
Earl of Dysart Primary School, Grantham

Colours Of The Rainbow

Red
The rose in the garden smelling lovely and sweet
The ruby red ring shining in the sun
Strawberries juicy and lovely to eat.

Yellow
The sun is yellow bright in the sky
Flowers are yellow swaying and bright.

Pink
Lips are pink in the sun
Candyfloss is pink, blue and is sticky and sweet.

Green
Trees in the sun for me and everyone
Green grass in the garden for beetles to eat.

Purple
Purple plums from the garden, juicy for me to eat.

Orange
An orange is juicy and sweet for me to eat.

Blue
The sky is blue up high in the sky
The sea is blue with fish and squid.

Lilly Newhouse (8)
Earl of Dysart Primary School, Grantham

The Colours Of The Rainbow

Roses have a nice smell, they are red and bright.
Cherries are juicy, delicious and tasty to eat.
Rubies are bright and shiny through your eyes.

The sun is bright, shiny and hot.
A sunflower makes me sneeze.
A canary is a bird and is loud, sitting in a tree.

A pig is loud with a curly tail.
A flamingo stands on one leg.
My pink dress, nice for girls to wear.
Pink lipstick which looks good on a lady's lips.

Grass swaying in the breeze.
A frog jumping and loud and has lots of energy.
Trees swaying side to side like they are walking.

An amethyst is good for ladies.
A wizard's hat, pointy, sharp and magic.
A purple potion that makes me fly like a bird.

The flaming fire which is very, very hot.
A sunset is when the sun goes to bed.
An orange is very juicy and delicious and tasty.

The sky full with clouds and birds.
An ocean is wet and warm and cold.
A dolphin has sharp teeth, it swims in the water.

Aiste Stankeviciute (9)
Earl of Dysart Primary School, Grantham

The Colours Of The Rainbow

A cherry is juicy, delicious and tasty to eat.
A rose can be good to use at your wedding.
A ruby necklace hanging in a jewellery shop.

The sun bright, very hot and shiny on our house.
A sunflower smells nicer and has got black seeds.
A canary flying over your homes.

A pig has a curly tail and is fat.
A flamingo is a little bit fat and pink.
Lipstick is soft, smooth and pink.

Grass is long, sometimes light and sometimes dark.
A crocodile has sharp teeth and is long.
Emeralds are green.

A wizard's hat is pointy, big and purple.
A wizard's cloak is long and shiny.
A potion is hot and makes you bigger.

A fire is hot, big and makes you go very hot.
The sunset is bright, big and sometimes goes yellow.
Goldfish are small, orange and live in water.
A starfish lives in the sea, sometimes small and sometimes big.

Bluebells are light and bent over.
The ocean is salty, sharks live in it.
A dolphin swims in the sea.

Helen McLardy (9)
Earl of Dysart Primary School, Grantham

The Colours Of The Rainbow

Red
A lovely, sparkling ruby that would fit on a lady's finger.
A juicy, delicious cherry on top of a tasty ice cream.
Roses smell nice and perfect on a Wednesday.
Lips are lovely, red lips on your face.

Yellow
Yellow sunflowers look at the sun and are sparkly.
Lions are fierce and scary, but nice and yellow.
The sun is nice and hot like fire.

Pink
Pigs are fat and smelly, but lovely and pink.
A flamingo is a bird that eats fish and is very pretty.

Green
The grass is green and swishes like a fish's fins.
Emeralds sparkling on your finger, neck and wrist.

Purple
An amethyst is pretty.
A purple potion to give you wings.
A wizard's cloak to put on your back and give you power.

Orange
Fire is hot and burns when you go near it.
Sunsets are pretty and orange.
Goldfish are orange and swim in water.

Blue
Bluebells are flowers. They are really pretty and smell nice.
The ocean is blue and very wet.
The sky is sometimes cloudy, but beautiful.

Gold
In this world, there is lots and lots of gold money.
Crowns are made of gold with jewels in them.

Silver
Metal is made of silver, you can make lots of things out of it.
Earrings are silver with sparkly things.

Fae Blake (8)
Earl of Dysart Primary School, Grantham

Colours Of The Rainbow

Dragon's flame burning trees,
A rose swishing in the wind,
A strawberry in a strawberry field.

Bees flying in the air,
Butterflies fluttering into summer breeze.
Canaries flying everywhere.

Candyfloss is icky and sticky,
Blossoms swishing in the wind,
Pretty flamingo standing on one leg.

Green grass swishing in the wind,
Leaves swinging in the summer breeze,
A face like a zombie.

Nathan Smith (8)
Earl of Dysart Primary School, Grantham

The Colours Of The Rainbow

Red
Dragon's red scales with spiky tail,
Dragon's flames hot and bright,
Blood flowing through our veins.

Yellow
Bright yellow paint in the big can,
The sunflowers dancing in the powerful wind.

Pink
The little pig rolling in the mud,
The pink gems on the Queen's crown,
The lovely pink candyfloss sticking to my face.

Green
The green juicy apple growing on the tree,
The green grass growing on the field,
The funny jelly beans jumping happily.

Purple
The deep dark plum in my mouth,
The purple grapes hanging from the tree.

Jorge Goncalves (9)
Earl of Dysart Primary School, Grantham

The Colours Of The Rainbow

Red
Cherry - juicy, delicious and tasty to eat.
Ruby - a ring around the Queen's finger.
Rose - a red rose so beautiful that you would be able to take it to
a wedding.

Pink
Pig - a pink pig with a curly tail.
Flamingo - a pink bird that can't fly.
Lipstick - a beautiful colour that you can wear when you go out.

Yellow
Sun - shining in the light, blue sky.
Fire - shining and shimmering in the light.
Sunflower - swaying side to side in the wind.

Purple
Amethyst - a beautiful stone
Wizard's cloak - a nice cloak with stars on
Potion - a precious liquid to drink.

Green
Grass - that you can look at on the ground.
Crocodile - a mean creature.
Grasshopper - a friendly creature that hops around.

Orange
Sun - a bright colour.
Fire - a hot flame.
Goldfish - a shiny fish.

Blue
Bluebells - sweet and pretty to see.
Ocean - a nice see-through colour.
Dolphin - a nice and amazing animal.

Kyarna Priest (8)
Earl of Dysart Primary School, Grantham

The Colours Of The Rainbow

A rose is red, bright, delicious, a delight.
Strawberries are red, ready to pick and easy to eat.
Blood flowing through your stomach.
Cherries, juicy, delicious to eat.
A ruby shining through your eyes.

The sun is as bright as the sand.
A sunflower is as bright as a golden mask.
A canary, like the sun, is flying around.

A pink dress, girls wear them all the time.
A flamingo standing on its leg for hours.
Lipstick that girls also wear, I just can't stand it!

Grass going this way, that way.
A crocodile snapping its teeth.
Frogs, they go mad when they see something grey.
Trees blowing as hard as they can.
Chameleons changing colours every day.

An amethyst in a gold ring.
A wizard's cloak shining.
A potion swirling around.

The sun ready to go down.
Goldfish sparkling all around a pond.
A fire, flames up high.

The ocean, as smooth as ice,
A dolphin jumping up and down.
The sky, you could watch it all day.

Grayson Barnes (9)
Earl of Dysart Primary School, Grantham

The Colours Of The Rainbow

Roses are scented with a beautiful smell.
Strawberries, tasty, light and bright.
Sunrise can be seen in the sky.

A banana is yellow, tasty and bright.
Sunflowers with shimmering petals swaying in the breeze.
Bee stripes, yellow and brilliant.

Candyfloss so light and sticky.
Pig, pink, dirty with a curly tail.
Flamingos stand and sleep.

Green grass standing in a row.
Apple skin shiny and green.
Cabbage leaves all around.

Grated carrot in a sandwich.

Grapes are purple and delicious.
Plum juice is sweet.

The ocean is blue.
The sky above me is blue.

Jodie Finney (8)
Earl of Dysart Primary School, Grantham

The Colours Of The Rainbow

The roses are red, and have a smell.
Poppies are nice and are sweet.
Rubies are red and shine like glass.
Strawberries are sweet and are so juicy.

The sun is yellow and so bright.
A sunflower is nice and so lovely.
A banana is so nice and tasty.
The moon is so bright.
A bee's stripes are yellow as they buzz in the light.

The heart is so pink in a body.
A pig is pink with a pink tail.
The flamingo is pink as it stands on one leg.
Candyfloss is pink and sticky.

The grass is swishing in the wind.
A big apple has been eaten from a house.
A leaf is hanging from a tree for the giraffes.
The seaweed is in the sea and flowing.

The goldfish is orange in the fish tank.
The carrot is nice and juicy.
An orange is so bright and orange.

The dolphin swimming in the sea.
The sky is so bright and lovely.

Ellie-Mae Brown (8)
Earl of Dysart Primary School, Grantham

Colours Of The Rainbow

Cherries are juicy, delicious and tasty to eat.
Ruby earrings, necklaces, we all wear them.
Roses smelling so sweet.

The sun is shiny, bright and hot.
Sunflowers are swaying side to side.
A canary flying high in the bright blue sky.

A pig is mucky and fat.
A flamingo stands on one leg for hours.
A dress, a bright pink dress with flowers on.
Lipstick is soft and pink.

Grass is long, short and sometimes dark and sometimes light.
A crocodile has sharp teeth and a long thin tail.
A frog is bouncy and green.

A wizard's hat is pointy and big.
A wizard's cloak is long with lots of stars on it.
A potion to make you fly or shrink.

A fire is hot with red and yellow flames.
The sunset is beautiful and lovely.
Goldfish are fast, swimming in the pond.

Bluebells are blue and swaying.
The ocean is big.
A dolphin is blue, big and slow.

Rhiann Moir (8)
Earl of Dysart Primary School, Grantham

The Colours Of The Rainbow

Red
Roses are a beautiful scent to smell.
Strawberries are scrumptious, shiny and juicy, also red as blood.
Cherries are as shiny as a polished apple when eaten by a princess.

Yellow
The sun is hot, yellow and goldy as a unicorn's horn shining like a gold ring.
A daffodil is yellow, soft and has a wonderful smell.
A canary has feathery wings as soft as polar bears' fur.

Pink
A flamingo is feathery, soft pink as a sparkling lipgloss stand,
Blush is powdery, soft and dusty like an old treasure map.

Green
An emerald is as shiny and sparkly as a reflecting mirror,
The grass is thin, smooth and shiny, swaying in the wind.
A crocodiile is green, scary and bumpy like a dinosaur catching its prey.

Purple
A potion is as smoky and black like a wizard's cauldron bubbling up In the night
Lipstick is as shiny and reflecting like a mirror that a witch is about to talk to,
An amethyst is as sparkly as the ocean in the sunset.

Blue
The sky is blue as a butterfly flying in the background,
A bluebird is as sweet as a rose swishing and swaying,
The sea is as blue and sparkly as a sapphire.

Leah McGhee (9)
Earl of Dysart Primary School, Grantham

The Web

(Inspired by 'The Sea' by Alice Barwell)

Scurrying, scuttling, scampering
As he spirals the victim on his delicate, stifling web.

He was slyly creeping and crawling along the web,
He felt guilty inside but approached and eagerly wanted to attack,
No sound could be heard apart from the leaves crackling off the trees
With his evil bulgy eyes staring.

Launching, leering, lingering
Anxiously wanting to attack his victim.

He was slyly creeping and crawling along the web,
He felt guilty inside but approached and eagerly wanted to attack,
No sound could be heard apart from the leaves crackling off the trees
With his evil bulgy eyes staring.

Devouring, destroying, defeating
As he poisons the fearing prey in a gloomy den.

A blood trail led to where the bully had attacked!

Honor Drummond (10)
Great Doddington Primary School, Wellingborough

The Web Of Doom

(Inspired by 'The Sea' by Alice Barwell)

Writhing, whirling, waiting.
He waits philosophically for his victim to come near.

The predator positions himself artfully.
His stomach churns in spasms as he slowly licks his lips in
anticipation.
His heart beating furiously as the footsteps get louder.
His nostrils flare in victorious conquest.

Threatening, traumatising, tormenting.
He slyly approaches his victim in unaware doom.

The predator positions himself artfully.
His stomach churns in spasms as he slowly licks his lips in
anticipation.
His heart beating furiously as the footsteps get louder.
His nostrils flare in victorious conquest.

Screaming, screeching, seducing.
His victim writhes in blood-curdling pain.

The bully strides out to war.

Kirby Carter (11)
Great Doddington Primary School, Wellingborough

No Escape

(Inspired by 'The Sea' by Alice Barwell)

Loitering, lingering, lurking
He waits in a creepy dark corner.

He slowly approaches his prey
He's feeling excited and important as he gets nearer
It's as silent as midnight on a cold winter's day
He looks joyful and excited the closer he gets.

Scuttling, slipping, scampering
Running towards his prey with blistering pace.

He slowly approaches his prey
He's feeling excited and important as he gets nearer
It's as silent as midnight on a cold winter's day
He looks joyful and excited the closer he gets.

Creeping, crawling, capturing
He silently sneaks up on his victim.

The bully catches his prey and beats him ferociously.

Sean Sinfield (10)
Great Doddington Primary School, Wellingborough

Terror Predator

(Inspired by 'The Sea' by Alice Barwell)

Terrifying, terrorising, teasing.
He lurks in dark corners waiting for his prey.

Creeping, wriggling he moves silently so as not to be seen.
His heart pounding with excitement as he finds his victim.
Silently moving, positioning himself in the trapping shadows
Ready to pounce.
Smirking thoughts of his weak and fragile victim engulf his face.

Growling, gulping, gruelling.
He lurches and lunges around his territory.

Creeping, wriggling he moves silently so as not to be seen.
His heart pounding with excitement as he finds his victim.
Silently moving, positioning himself in the trapping shadows ready to pounce.
Smirking thoughts of his weak and fragile victim engulf his face.

Punching, pinching, plunging.
The helpless creature screams, trapped by his predator.

The vicious, aggressive bully leaves his helpless victim after one more fearful strike.

Matthew Parsons (10)
Great Doddington Primary School, Wellingborough

No Escape

(Inspired by 'The Sea' by Alice Barwell)

Climbing, creating, crawling
He makes his sinister trap for his victim.

Scuttling across his deadly trap.
He can feel his heart pounding as he creeps towards his victim.
All he hears is a slow muttering coming from his hesitant prey.
He scrunches his eyes together as he gets ready to pounce.

Dashing, darting, defeating
He jumps for his helpless victim.

Scuttling across his deadly trap.
He can feel his heart pounding as he creeps towards his victim.
All he hears is a slow muttering coming from his hesitant prey.
He scrunches his eyes together as he gets ready to pounce.

Snapping, sneering, snatching
He destroys his victim's terrified mind and fragile body.

The bully catches his prey.

Lauren Wood (10)
Great Doddington Primary School, Wellingborough

Hunted

(Inspired by 'The Sea' by Alice Barwell)

Spinning, sneaking, seeking
The victim is unaware.

The hunter moves stealthily
He feels the presence of his victim
He hears the light footsteps as his victim approaches almost silently
nearer
An evil sneer appears on his face as he pounces on his victim.

Intimidating, immobilising, intoxicating
Poison dripping from the fangs.

The hunter moves stealthily
He feels the presence of his victim
He hears the light footsteps as his victim approaches almost silently
nearer
An evil sneer appears on his face as he pounces on his victim.

Thumping, taunting, terrifying
The victim has no chance.

The bully leaves him unconscious.

Elliott McLester (11)
Great Doddington Primary School, Wellingborough

Gotcha

(Inspired by 'The Sea' by Alice Barwell)

Spinning, sensing, smelling
Making his trap whilst hunting his prey.

He is sneakily creeping towards his prey, making sure he's unseen.
The prey is feeling scared - he senses there is a monster about.
The prey hears a rustle so he turns around but there's nothing there.
Saliva comes from his mouth as he pictures in his eyes the blood,
Guts and flesh from the victim.

Gripping, grabbing, grasping
He keeps out of sight, he's spotted his prey.

He is sneakily creeping towards his prey, making sure he's unseen.
The prey is feeling scared - he senses there is a monster about.
The prey hears a rustle so he turns around but there's nothing there.
Saliva comes from his mouth as he pictures in his eyes the blood,
Guts and flesh from the victim.

Terrorising, terrifying, tasting
He pounces, his gigantic body smothering his victim breathlessly.

The bully attacks.

Molly Underwood (11)
Great Doddington Primary School, Wellingborough

Spider

(Inspired by 'The Sea' by Alice Barwell)

Spinning, scaring, scraping,
Sneaking under beneath the dustbins.

He softly creeps towards his opponent,
Hesitant but excited,
Crunching his jaws in anticipation,
His eyes as big as his belly.

Rushing, rolling, rubbing.
He prances onto the web.

He softly creeps towards his opponent,
Hesitant but excited,
Crunching his jaws in anticipation,
His eyes as big as his belly.

Troubling, trying, terrifying.
He strikes and injures his prey.

The bully struts away smirking, leaving the victim with his injuries.

Lawrence Jefferies (10)
Great Doddington Primary School, Wellingborough

The Web

(Inspired by 'The Sea' by Alice Barwell)

Tasting, tempting, teasing
Staying low underneath a smelly garbage bin.

He tiptoes across the lines
Feeling anxious to get his teeth into something or someone.
He could hear the sound of his victim coming down the dark, damp alleyway.
His face had a huge smirk on it - the time was drawing near.

Repulsing, rearing, raging
He leaps aggressively upon his victim.

He tiptoes across the lines
Feeling anxious to get his teeth into something or someone.
He could hear the sound of his victim coming down the dark, damp alleyway.
His face had a huge smirk on it - the time was drawing near.

Lingering, launching, liquidising
He devours and crunches his dupe.

The bully scampers across the road with the victim's lunch money.

Amarn Rowe (10)
Great Doddington Primary School, Wellingborough

There's No Escape

(Inspired by 'The Sea' by Alice Barwell)

Creeping, clutching, crushing.
Lurking in a gloomy corner waiting to pounce on his victim.

He scuttles into a murky corner ready to pounce.
Waiting anxiously to sink his teeth into the enemy.
Crawling cautiously after the figure, making no sound at all.
Glaring at his foe ready to harm him.

Seizing, savaging, snatching.
Grasping its prey and crushing it just for fun.

He scuttles into a murky corner ready to pounce.
Waiting anxiously to sink his teeth into the enemy.
Crawling cautiously after the figure, making no sound at all.
Glaring at his foe ready to harm him.

Devouring, destroying, daring.
Demolishing the prey as he goes down, he is victorious.

The bully dashes away, feeling proud of himself.

Jack Greenacre (11)
Great Doddington Primary School, Wellingborough

Spider Trap

(Inspired by 'The Sea' by Alice Barwell)

Waiting, watching, wondering,
He lurks in the thorn bush.

Waiting for his victim.
Creeping forward as quiet as a mouse.
His heart is beating faster and faster.
His whole body is ready.

Spinning, sneaking, suffering,
Gets in a good position and jumps on his victim.

Waiting for his victim.
Creeping forward as quiet as a mouse.
His heart is beating faster and faster.
His whole body is ready.

Preparing, prompting, pulverising,
The enemy screams.

And the bully runs away.

John Davies (10)
Great Doddington Primary School, Wellingborough

Trapped

(Inspired by 'The Sea' by Alice Barwell)

Lurking, looming, lunching
Hiding in a creepy corner.

He creeps stealthily towards his victim
Quivering excitedly in anticipation
The leaves quietly rustling under his feet
An evil smirk glides across his face.

Creeping, chasing, catching
Sprinting towards his helpless victim.

He creeps stealthily towards his victim
Quivering excitedly in anticipation
The leaves quietly rustling under his feet
An evil smirk glides across his face.

Degrading, destroying, devouring
He finally catches his prey.

The bully walks off, leaving his victim with blood dripping down
his face.

Jodie Summers (10)
Great Doddington Primary School, Wellingborough

Eleanor Rigby
(Inspired by The Beatles)

Bobby McKenzie
Turning the key of the door on his cold empty house
No one about
Tears fall from his eyes
Rolling slowly down the cheeks of his sad, lonely face
It's not a disgrace.

Oliver Chatterton (10)
Great Doddington Primary School, Wellingborough

The River's Journey

The journey is a voyage,
It's wet and wild!
Sometimes you see it flow.
But I promise you that some bits will be mild.

The river is a-trickling,
Down from the mountain pool.
It's slow and calm,
But then it comes to a great fall!

The river is a-tumbling,
Down from a waterfall.
It cascades with strength to spit and spray,
The water is very clean and cool.

The river is escorting,
Water ever growing,
Accompanying the calm waves of the river,
Strangely the water's still flowing.

The river is a-churning,
Dirt and water ever mixing,
There are banks full of deposits,
The seas are ever fixing.

The river is a voyage
Of trickling, tumbling, escorting and churning
Out to sea.

Brad Baines (10)
High Ash CE Combined School, Great Brickhill

A Journey To The Sea

The river is a large stream of cool water,
Flowing in a natural channel.
It starts in the mountains and ends in the sea.
Maybe it could start smooth and end rough.

First of all it could be twisting and turning.
It begins in the distant mountains.
The river trickles and tickles down the slope.
Also the water flows side to side.

Then it splashes and sprays strongly over rocks.
The water cascades everywhere.
It rushes and tumbles powerfully round bends.
Although it flips and rolls everywhere.

The tributaries accompany the river.
It rolls and wriggles and it rises.
It meanders slowly into every place.
The white water is full of rhythm.

The rough gradient is rushing and racing.
It looks quite pretty and spectacular.
The river carries sediment along too.
It is hazardous and dangerous.

The water twists and turns down every pathway.
The river is a torrential flow.
It deposits sediment on the inside.
It finally reaches the cool sea.

First of all the river is in the mountains.
Then it cascades down and over rocks.
After that lots of tributaries join on too.
Finally it is an overflow.

Lucy Billington (10)
High Ash CE Combined School, Great Brickhill

The River

The massive flow of water,
Just like it is never-ending,
Gathering more and more water,
The journey of a river ascending.

At the start it is only just beginning,
Bubbling, splashing and spurting,
Slow-moving, trickling and rippling,
Calm-moving only slightly splashing.

The energetic journey gets larger,
So if you fancy a float please take a boat!
As the epic travel becomes faster,
Don't go for a swim, please don't!

The calm river twirling,
Meandering side to side,
Swirling and whirling,
Becoming mild, still very wide.

Twisting, trying to find a place,
A place to deposit sand and rocks,
An extraordinary river has found an ample space,
The space of the sea.

Savannah Mercer (9)
High Ash CE Combined School, Great Brickhill

Journey

Trickle, trickle, trickle
Down the mountain edge,
A group of partridges fill the sky
Tu-whit, tu-whoo.

Torrential rapids over water,
Rolling, flowing water,
Carrying sand, the river journeys,
Swishing, gushing, rolling.

What's that in the far distance?
A long tributary!
White flowing water on the horizon,
Cascading over rocks.

Wider still, the river meanders,
Travelling, coves are made,
Mysteriously sand deposits,
Powerful, fast water.

Eventually the river fans out,
Islands are made, hundreds,
The water gets warmer,
Delta is all around.

Harriet Mahier (9)
High Ash CE Combined School, Great Brickhill

The River

The droplets fall in a Yorkshire pudding,
Like a big puddle,
They swirl around in circles,
They're in some sort of muddle.

They start to trickle out,
Of a little gap,
Tumbling onto rocks,
Somewhere there's got to be a tap!

And now it's started to narrow,
Like a big stick,
It is quite small now,
But I'm sure it will get thick!

There are lots of rocks and pebbles,
Laying around,
But they're wearing away,
By the water's powerful pound.

With a clash, a boom,
A bang and a creak,
Whooshing rapids,
Are starting to freak!

Stephanie Boad (9)
High Ash CE Combined School, Great Brickhill

The River

The river starts off as just a little trickle of water in a mountain
And it's as slow as a snail slithering.

The water then cascades
Over the rocks
Rubs away the rocks with all the small stones
Hazardous
The torrential rain raises the level of the water.

Then it calms down
Other streams join it
Tributary
Narrow, twisting water
Joining in.

The bending in the river
Makes the river meander
Sway like a shoelace twisting and meandering.

The river
Goes round
Small branches
To sea.

Owen Rickard (10)
High Ash CE Combined School, Great Brickhill

The River

The life of a river,
We all do know,
The path it takes,
Here wc go!

Tiny trickle,
Sunny stream,
Golden water,
Fiery gleam.

Becoming bigger
Faster too!
Raging rapids,
Big and blue.

Whining water,
Round the bend . . .
It looks so vast!
When will it end?

It's flowing freely,
Calmer now.
A tributary enters,
A giant tree bough.

The river's so muddy,
It's very slow.
It's dumped its mud,
It's stopped its flow.

And now we've reached the estuary,
We're actually very near the sea.

Alexander Ford (10)
High Ash CE Combined School, Great Brickhill

The River

The small flow gradually is getting stronger
Every second the greatness of a living flow
Blinded me from the greatness.

The swirly river made me dizzy
While I thought of the river
As a wheel spinning round and round grasping mud.

The river spinning
Like sharpenings of a pencil
Swirling round me.

A wave splashed all over me

The area was getting wider magically.

Barnaby Collins (9)
High Ash CE Combined School, Great Brickhill

The River

A smooth pebble,
A bubbly jacuzzi getting hotter and hotter,
The sandy tropical water trickles down the waterfall,
Through the rocky rapids,
Gradually getting deeper.

Rocks like crystals,
Water like sparkling rings,
Smelling all fruity,
In the loopy river.

It's getting stronger,
More crazy,
Ready to pounce out,
Whoosh here and there,
Boom, bang against the sides,
Like it's a massive fight.

It's windy,
The water is spraying,
It's going as quick as lightning,
Gush, flash, wallop goes the water,
All *whooshy* and bouncy.

Suddenly all calm,
It's all quiet,
The water is slow,
It's lovely!

Olly Margrave (9)
High Ash CE Combined School, Great Brickhill

The Mysterious River

At the peak of a mountain,
A trickle of water is tumbling down getting bigger and bigger.
Slipping through narrow pebbles.
Twirling like a ballerina and splashing against the cold hard rocks.

Looping over tributaries and winding past stones.
Sloshing and gurgling as it flows off the mountain.

Swift weird fish
Glide through the curling current
As mysterious birds swoop down and snap them up.
The water churns up as it skids and slides
Through thick green carpet.

The water swishes and swirls
As it carries huge boulders and leaps,
Dropping them
And it rushes back gushing and twisting
It crashes against the sheer rocky walls.
It whirls and roars and cascades
Downstream
People believe that
This mysterious river
Is on the other side of the world
And that it's in a wonderful land.

Jay Bowdler (9)
High Ash CE Combined School, Great Brickhill

The River

The river
A long stream of water
Flowing in a natural channel
Far up in the mountains it is a small stream
Trickling down slowly
A river is soft and cool and clear
It twists and turns from side to side.

The torrential water gushing everywhere
Splash! You can hear the water going up and down
Twirling, twisting, curling
That's the sound a river makes.

The mouth, a great huge alligator with three slippery rocks.

Rolling, swirling and rotating
That's the sound a river makes.

Bradley Watts (9)
High Ash CE Combined School, Great Brickhill

Rivers

This long journey will take you through a tropical place.
A small stream starts from a
Mountain as high as a tower and
Makes its way down,
It cascades down hills and
Tumbles over rocks like snow
Falling from the sky and rolled into
A snowball.

The water rushes rapidly,
Tributaries join the river as well
As stones and rocks,
Torrents of water come and go
And sweep the riverbed clean.

The water meanders like a car
Out of control,
The water goes from side to side
Making small beaches on the way.

The water dodges the delta like a
Soldier dodging bullets,
Finally it reaches the mouth of its journey.

James Blaesbjerg (10)
High Ash CE Combined School, Great Brickhill

The River

What is a river?
Stormy, tumbling blue,
Swirls, energetic white,
Or gentle see-through.

Up in the mountains,
High in the sky,
Rippling, calm, trickling,
A river goes by.

Along comes a stream,
Joins gracefully along,
(Also enlarged by rain)
Fitting together like a song.

Torrential, flowing,
Cascades, many rocks,
White water, energy found,
Everything could not block.

Forceful water meanders
Softly from side to side,
Sometimes very narrow or
Occasionally wide.

Along the green carpets,
The river now glides,
Depositing sediment,
To where it can hide.

Alone at night in dark,
Often twists and turns,
Sadly nowhere to go,
Travels just where it yearns . . .

Abigail West (10)
High Ash CE Combined School, Great Brickhill

The River

An overflowing bath,
A river made in the rock,
Freezing water is gone,
It goes through the village.

More water comes through,
The tributaries like snakes,
Little fish in the river.

It approaches the sea,
It gets bigger and bigger,
You can see the boats.

And the waves in the sea,
Are crashing onto the beach.

Robert Valledy (10)
High Ash CE Combined School, Great Brickhill

River Flow

A trickling tap,
Rainwater falls,
Gently swerving,
Edge to edge.

Roller coaster ahead,
Plunging away,
Pointy rocks on the cliff edge,
Calming, soothing river.

Churning, moody moving motorway,
Forest above my head,
Animals are now coming,
Snakes are in trees,
Fish are in the water.

Daylight you can see,
White water oncoming,
A plane out of control,
Meandering is going on,
People twisting side to side
In the narrow boat.

Mountain surroundings,
Flat custard lake,
Gravy in the middle
Of a Yorkshire pudding,
Salty water heading to sea.

Antonia Leech (9)
High Ash CE Combined School, Great Brickhill

The River

As the flowing river begins,
It harmlessly shoves,
Objects out of its way,
A long, white piece of silk.

The tributaries join to the gleaming river,
Like families and friends being reunited,
Meandering rapids take over the river.

Feathered friends stare at the scaly fish,
Thinking they're for dinner!
The fish do not know,
All they ever do is dart up and down,
The lengthy river!

The giant mouth opens and the river goes through,
Not knowing where it is going,
Splash here, splash there,
Over the noisy river!

Anna Irwin (9)
High Ash CE Combined School, Great Brickhill

The River

As it begins to drop,
It's plain to see,
After every tributary,
Thc way it grows.
Dribbling down the steep rockface,
The water falls,
The ground below calls,
Like a tap half-on, it trickles.

It starts to get quicker,
The noise is getting louder,
As it comes down the mountain, it looks like talcum powder,
Where is it going to? We'll soon find out.

As it comes to the bottom, the momentum takes over,
It's churning and crashing,
And cascading and splashing,
It's getting calmer now, let's follow its path.

It's looping like a scarf,
Meandering in and out,
It's like a funnel, how it grows, home to many trout.

Watch out! Be careful! Here comes the rapids!

The rocks are like sharks,
The dangerous currents could kill,
And I'm starting to feel ill!
Oh no! I've fallen out the boat!

Phew! It's okay, it's getting calmer now,
It's a mirror, I can see myself, hello!
The river's splitting up now, which way do I go?
Let's go to the right, it's wider there.

I've kept on going, crossroads ahead,
I can go left, right or centre,
Or diagonally instead,
We're at the sea now; I'm going to relax on the beach.
Phew!

Danny Burke (9)
High Ash CE Combined School, Great Brickhill

The River

A tall peak,
A small trickle of a stream,
Faster, gathering momentum,
Running, running, running,
Running down the mountainside.

A drop slide hurtling down,
Onto a mountain ledge,
Cascading over rocks,
Swirling with God's full power,
Gushing, gushing, gushing,
Gushing round bumpy rocks.

A breaking car screeching to a halt,
With piranhas like a misty cloud,
An eternal resource,
Flowing, flowing, flowing,
Flowing through dense jungle.

Down again,
A spluttering car,
Full of life,
Roaring, roaring, roaring,
Roaring round tiny villages.

Spitting serpent heads,
A Devil's fork,
Piles of sand abandoned,
Crashing, crashing, crashing,
Crashing along the ocean floor . . .

Harry Renson (10)
High Ash CE Combined School, Great Brickhill

The River!

The river,
Something with hidden secrets down below,
Clashing, bashing between the rocks,
Gushing current swooping things up,
As it goes along the riverbed,
Swishing left to right like trees in a forest.

The river,
Swirling, gurgling, splish, splosh, splashing,
As the river goes down the rock bashing,
Reflecting, gleaming in the sunlight,
Littering on the sides,
Smelling like an air freshener,
Fish in their natural habitat.

Fraser McGrath (9)
High Ash CE Combined School, Great Brickhill

The River

The clashing river
Tears the mountain
Like a lion exploring
Its prey.

A small path
There is for you to walk,
But only small
Or death becomes near.

Don't be worried
Because you're in shore,
So you're thankful for your home
(Unlike some people).

Sometimes the raging
And powerful river
Gives you peace
And is a romantic place like Heaven,
Although it meanders with,
Beauty it shall get deeper,
And deeper till it waves,
Like the wind blowing you away.

Samuel Hardwicke (9)
High Ash CE Combined School, Great Brickhill

The Lovely River

A pool of rain water,
Weakly trickling down a steep path,
Falling to words the pebbly surface.

The water travelling to somewhere wider,
Flowing gracefully along its path,
With tributaries joining.

Strong rapids force the boulders onto shore,
Fast water crashes and causes dents in the ground,
People risk going over the dangerous water,
Do you want to go over the noisy river?

As it gets closer to the sea it calms down,
The water calms,
And it gets wider,
Eventually reaches the sea.

Megan Searle (10)
High Ash CE Combined School, Great Brickhill

The River

The river, a trickling tap
A tiny channel surrounded by huge boulders,
A shallow puddle,
Down a massive hill,
Splashing against the rocks.

It gradually gets vast,
Tributaries connecting on,
Getting fast and faster,
As it travels.

It gets wider,
Rapids coming from all around,
Crashing down on the rocks,
Increasing speed.

It gets rougher and rougher,
Spraying up into the air,
Making funny noises.

Calming down,
Swaying from side to side,
Gradually getting shallower,
As it reaches the sea.

Turning into massive waves,
Crashing onto the sand,
Again, again and again.

It gradually changes direction,
And travels out to sea.

Ryan Watts (9)
High Ash CE Combined School, Great Brickhill

The River

Splashing, twirling, rushing, diving snake.
Jumping little creatures
Inside the magnificent snake's belly.
Looping in and out of trees
Which look like broccoli
And boulders like huge tortoises.
People having picnics
On the emerald-green grass.
Young children having a swim
In the crystal-clear blue waters,
Splashing around in the hot blazing sun.
A frozen rock
Sparkling in the hot, burning fireball
In the sky.
A frothy waterfall in the sun
Like crystals falling into
A golden pool of diamonds.

Emily Whittall (9)
High Ash CE Combined School, Great Brickhill

Rivers!

High up in the mountain
A little drop of water can make a huge difference to the world
Because that little drop can form into a massive river!

A little trickle tumbling down,
About to enter the ride of its lifetime.

Cascading and twisting,
Looking for more room like a spaceman.

Raging rapids lashing out into the air, like a tiger!

A great whale opening its spout,
Ready to shoot the air.

It is now powerful like a digger, going over or around
Anything in its path.
You now know a river, mighty and strong!
Yes, yes it is a river indeed.

Hollie Canham (9)
High Ash CE Combined School, Great Brickhill

River

A river running, rippling along will eventually find itself
Meeting mighty sea.

It starts up as tall as the clouds as a small, slow, smooth
Stream of water,
This is just beginning to fall gently towards the bottom.

Dribbling along, getting faster now, with more speed,
Some tiny trickling tributaries push themselves to the big one,
Narrow, is getting bigger now.

Now it has reached the bottom,
It's a torrent of water smashing itself in a gush,
The river rushing rapidly through the valley, cascading
Over rocks, lashing against stones in a tumble.

The river eventually becomes wide and gentle,
With the current calmly carrying itself along,
It's a-flowing and twisting between a green carpet of trees.

Now the river has met its end, it has united with the sea,
Shifting, shuffling sand dropping down to make beautiful sandbanks,
The river will separate but come together to meet the sea.

Harry Strong (9)
High Ash CE Combined School, Great Brickhill

Tower In Portsmouth

If Dad stood on a tower in Portsmouth he wouldn't know what to do,
He would freak out and scream with fright and he is scared
of heights too.

Because you go up and up and up and see how high you are,
You look up to the sparkling night sky above you and see
a little bright star.

But he looks down through the solid glass floor and feels
a little bit alone,
All the chatting people are far below him and he's up there on his own.

Cameron Arkley (6)
Holtspur School, Beaconsfield

The Hungry Croc

There once was a hungry crocodile,
Who lived in the river Nile.
He ate a cat,
And got terribly fat,
And stayed off food for a while.

Matthew Smout (9)
Holtspur School, Beaconsfield

Kangaroo

There once was a bouncy kangaroo
He lived in an enormous zoo.
He ate lots of honey
He never had any money
And jumped with his body too.

Laurren Bowler (8)
Holtspur School, Beaconsfield

A Man Called Bill

There once was a man called Bill
Who worked a Tesco till
He jumped out of bed
Bumped his head
So he stayed off work because he was ill.

Kelsie Elliott (9)
Holtspur School, Beaconsfield

Escape!

There was a young kangaroo,
Who escaped from London Zoo.
He thought he was cool,
But he was really a fool
Because he caused such a hullabaloo!

Chloe Rees Pearman (8)
Holtspur School, Beaconsfield

The Boy From The North

There was a young boy from the north,
Who found out his dad was a dwarf.
When he entered a race,
He couldn't show his face,
'Cause his dad didn't even come fourth!

Sarah Clark (9)
Holtspur School, Beaconsfield

The Unlucky Boy

There once was a boy who lived at a zoo
Whose job was to look after kangaroos
He went into one's cage
It had a terrible rage
And now the boy is covered in poo.

Alistair Beard (9)
Holtspur School, Beaconsfield

Billy

There once was a boy called Billy
Who could be extremely silly
He didn't like work
It drove him berserk
That lazy young boy called Billy.

Billy Cochrane (9)
Holtspur School, Beaconsfield

You Funny Bunny

There once was a very big bunny
Who was incredibly funny
He showed his friend
Who got the wrong end
Now he is trying to get some money.

Matthew Foster (9)
Holtspur School, Beaconsfield

Brown Kangaroo!

There once was a kangaroo in a zoo
Who instead of being brown was blue
He wanted to be brown
It really made him frown
That poor unlucky kangaroo.

Aiya Flatman (8)
Holtspur School, Beaconsfield

The Man In The War

There once was a man in the war
Who was very poor
He went in a ditch
And got very rich
And now he's not poor anymore.

Connor Jackson (9)
Holtspur School, Beaconsfield

Owen

There was a young boy called Owen
Who didn't know where he was goin'
One day he found his way
And shouted hooray!
Now Owen knows where he is goin'.

Owen Galera (8)
Holtspur School, Beaconsfield

A Naughty Kangaroo

There was a kangaroo
Who escaped from London Zoo,
Who hopped down the lane,
A woman fainted in pain,
A cheetah followed along too.

Lulu Pratt (9)
Holtspur School, Beaconsfield

Biscuit Taster

I can smell a new set of delicious warm chocolate cookies,
Ready to be tasted by professionals
I can hear my teeth grabbing it, like a digger taking a mouth of earth
But at the same time I can still smell the melting caramel in the
biscuit.
I can taste the glorious coconut amongst the digestives
I can see the pink icing dancing on the biscuit.
I can taste the hard crisp hazelnuts sticking in my teeth
And I can taste the soft cushion like raisins.
I can smell the coffee vapours wafting up my nose
I can see the smooth ripples staying exactly as they had been
modelled.
I can hear the loud booming sound as I crunch the biscuit
I can feel the melted chocolate oozing down my throat
With the sweet crumbly shortbread chasing it down.

Holly Tucker (9)
Molescroft Primary School, Beverley

Anger

Anger is red like Hell,
Living in a cell.
It steams like burning rock,
It looks like ashes from your gran burning ashes.
It sounds like heavy crackling,
It feels like burning sticky rock,
It tastes like boiling sticky mustard
It reminds me of fire burning in Hell!

Trent Woodley (8)
Park Junior School, Wellingborough

Fly High Butterfly - Haikus

Fly high butterfly,
And show your pretty colours,
As you fly up high.

Swim fast little fish,
As you glide through the blue sea,
Scales sparkly bright.

Bark loud furry dog,
Your fur shimmers in the sun,
With your waggy tail.

Amy Gardner (11)
Putteridge Junior School, Luton

Football

Football, football,
We all love you, goalies and strikers,
Midfielders and defenders
Running down the pitch, getting closer and closer,
Until the moment comes,
The crowd goes silent,
Wait for it, wait for it,
Shoot
And
Score!

Shannon Williams (10)
Putteridge Junior School, Luton

My Maths Teacher Is Evil

My maths teacher is evil
She comes from the planet Mars
She bombards us with sums and subtractions
And puts all our spirits in jars.

My maths teacher is evil
She makes all the little ones cry
With minus numbers and addition
And a glare which could make you die!

My maths teacher is evil
She's always on my case
She makes my life a misery
And she definitely came from space!

Sian Shannon-Sinclair (11)
Putteridge Junior School, Luton

Things That Make Us Happy

Chocolate brownies and ice cream sundaes
Holiday treats and special fun days
Light blue skies that dazzle your eyes
Birthday cake and hot apple pies
Roses so bright they could ruin your sight
Swimming with dolphins in blue crystal light
Playing with puppy dogs joyful and snappy
These are the things that can make us happy.

Lara Burton (10)
Putteridge Junior School, Luton

Horses

I have a special love,
Not an ant or a dove,
But what I really love is,
Horses!

The way they look at you when you smile,
The way they put the hay in a pile,
But when you ride them you can see,
How wonderful horses can really be!

Sometimes they're naughty, sometimes they're good,
But you'll always get them to behave like they should,
You can ride in the rain, wind, snow or sun,
But you'll always certainly have lots of fun!

But when it's time to say goodbye,
You might even nearly cry,
Because all the fun you've had that day,
Will stay in your heart and never go away!

Amy Pollard (11)
Putteridge Junior School, Luton

Flowers

Flowers, flowers, they're so bright
They are so beautiful in the sunlight
The birds whistle and chirp their song
All the while the grass grows long.

The roses glow a radiant red
While the bees collect honey from the flower bed
Autumn rolls in and the leaves turn brown
And they fall off the trees and litter the ground.

Kiera Hobbs (10)
Putteridge Junior School, Luton

Space

S tars shining as bright as the sun
P lanets far, far away that mankind cannot reach
A stronauts trying to be the first to discover a new planet
C omets flying through time and space not knowing where they
will land
E ven the latest technology cannot take people to the edge of space
and it never will.

Ben Evans (10)
Putteridge Junior School, Luton

I'll Be A Star One Day

I'll be a star one day,
Just you wait and see,
My name will be up in lights,
I'll be who I want to be.

I'll go on stage, sing my favourite song,
I'll act, and I'll play along,
I'll be at the Olympics, win a big prize,
I'll dance; I'll try costumes all on for size.

So what am I waiting for? I'm 11 years old,
I've got loads of time as I've been told,
So just watch out, you will see my show,
Sit back, relax and then you'll know,
Don't just sit there, get up and go!

Lucy Jefferies (11)
Putteridge Junior School, Luton

The Lost Homework

That one day I lost my book,
I had lost it so I had to look.
I looked in every nook and cranny,
I even had to call my granny.

I looked in here and I looked up there,
But I couldn't look, oh no, I wouldn't dare.
To look in the room where my sister sleeps,
Because she hurts all the ones who dare to peep.

In the end I found it next to the tree
In the garden with a bee.
I knew who put it there, oh yes I did,
My little sister called Orchid.

Mark Waterhouse (10)
Putteridge Junior School, Luton

Alfie

My brother,
My best friend,
My partner in crime,
My buddy,
My mate,
My reason to rhyme.

I love him,
I like him,
I want him to be,
My best friend forever,
And all eternity.

He's funny,
He's smart,
He's cool like no other,
He's clever,
He's kind,
He is my brother.

Jack Dinsey (10)
Putteridge Junior School, Luton

Fantasy World

Make-believe pixies,
Little green elves,
Bursts out from the stories,
My grandparents tell.

Little round brownies,
With incredibly long beards,
And tiny, dainty fairies,
To cast away your fears.

Short, muscular gnomes,
Dig, hoping for treasure,
Any kind of rare find,
Gives them great pleasure.

Cruel, wicked goblins,
With long, old twined fingers,
Live in gruesome places,
Where trouble lingers.

Just then in the distance,
You sense a rumbling roar,
As giants and trolls
Thump huge feet on the floor.

Evil-eyed sorcerers,
Whiz through crisp night air
Tricking helpless young rabbits
Into their lairs.

Fantasy world,
Only comes in your dreams,
So shut your eyes tightly,
Then you'll see!

Ellie Hudson (10)
Putteridge Junior School, Luton

The Game Boy

My brother is a game addict,
He loves to play all day.
One day he played two days straight,
Obviously I had to wait.

My brother is a game addict,
He loves to win all the time.
Whenever we beat him,
He thinks we've made a sin.

My brother is a game addict,
He loves to watch TV.
Whenever we hold the remote control,
He acts like an angry troll.

Kyle Grizzell (10)
Putteridge Junior School, Luton

Katie, My Best Friend

Katie
Katie's always funny
But she's not a hunny bunny
She likes skeletons and bones
And she never ever moans
Her favourite animal is a shark
And she likes going to the park
She has ginger hair
And she doesn't care
But she's my best friend
And she will be till the end
That's Katie
My best friend.

Ellie Chittenden (9)
Putteridge Junior School, Luton

Me

I am
A fast smooth-running orange McLaren F1
An orange and black striking corn snake
A wobbly and bouncy jelly
A sharpener, sharpening all those blunt pencils
A rubber, so I can rub out all the things I don't like
A bubbly and fizzy Diet Coke
A dark orange bouncy chair.

Sebastian Cooper (10)
Putteridge Junior School, Luton

Swimming

I love swimming, it keeps me fit,
I swim at the speed of light,
I win gold and silver medals,
It's my favourite thing.

I'm better than my friends,
I'm better than the best,
I'm a super swimmer,
But when I'm finished I go home for dinner!

Sophie Risbridger (10)
Putteridge Junior School, Luton

My Little Angel

My niece is an angel from
The sky
She's very sweet and very
Kind
She does her chores every day
Just like
A swift of a wave,
I said to her
One fine summer's day
You're my
Little angel who cares
About
Everyone every day.

Ibara Razaq (10)
Putteridge Junior School, Luton

Who Am I?

They made a song about me.
It was sung so beautifully, just like me.
People are constantly looking at me, admiring me.
They wrote a book about me.
They also made a film in my name.
I should be on the wall of fame.
I am very expensive.
I have a famous friend called Leonardo.
I am famous alongside other paintings.
I have an infectious smile.

Who am I?

I am Mona Lisa!

Harkirit Rayatt (9)
Putteridge Junior School, Luton

Zapperdude

Zapperdude flies in the sky,
And always makes the villains cry.
He fights evil day or night,
And has the power of X-ray sight.

With his bolts he can destroy,
Every bad man, girl or boy.
He tries to complete every task,
With his lucky orange mask.

With his short coal-black hair,
He has the courage to fight a bear.
He always defeats evil folk,
Then he goes home and drinks some Coke.

Alex Coles (10)
Putteridge Junior School, Luton

Earth

E arth is the big ball where life has come to be!
A s we know it, it holds the sky, land and sea!
R ight now I'm standing on it.
T he Earth's the bulb God lit.
H our by hour we're standing on it.
We should be thankful it's ours to share.

Bethany Freeman (10)
Putteridge Junior School, Luton

Footie

Footie, footie, that's the game
Who's your favourite, say the name . . .

Barca, Chelsea, Arsenal . . . Liverpool, oh of course
Man U's mine, they're the best
Far better than the rest.

Him and Liverpool, that's my friend
It really drives me round the bend
FA Cup soon, Liverpool will be gone
Man U v Liverpool, bring it on!
We disagree on it all the time
He thinks liking Man U is a crime.

Footie, footie, that's the game
Who's your favourite, say the name . . .

Stephen Osborne (10)
Putteridge Junior School, Luton

Football

F is for friends to play with
O is for being out in the fresh air
O is for outdoors fun
T is for tackling to win thc ball
B is for the ball, can't play without it!
A is for after school with your mates
L is for laughing with your friends
L is for loving the game.

Joe Perry (11)
Putteridge Junior School, Luton

Sunset

Red,
Orange,
Yellow,
The dazzling sun sets,
With beautiful bands of colour.
Into the horizon,
Disappearing from view,
In the middle of the cold,
Bitter winter.

Kim Fleming (11)
Ranskill Primary School, Retford

Winter Tree Poem

Winter trees standing alone,
Cold and bare,
Blowing in the wind,
Thin and unsteady.
Branches swaying side to side,
Trunk standing peacefully.
Hidden in a patch of mist,
Winter trees standing alone.

Rachael Wilkinson (10)
Ranskill Primary School, Retford

The Old Tree

Winter tree casting a shadow
in the sunlight.
Winter tree with your
long branches
watching over us
in the dark morning sky.
Staring at us with
your cold, naked eyes.

David Gough (10)
Ranskill Primary School, Retford

Winter Tree

Tall, thick trunk
in cold winter breeze,
Old twisted branches
creak in the snow-filled night.
Black branches filling a morning sky,
Standing alone in a brown field.

Abigail McMahon (9)
Ranskill Primary School, Retford

Fridays, Fridays

Fridays, Fridays are the worst,
I could really, really burst.

We go to the swimming pool,
I know it sounds cool getting out of school,
But I would rather be chased by a big, big bull.

I will tell you my reason why,
I can't ever, ever, ever get dry!

I come out with wet, wet hair,
It is never, ever, ever fair.

When it comes to getting dressed,
I'm not the very best.

So that's why Fridays are the worst,
And that's why I could really burst.

Mary MacDonald (9)
Ranskill Primary School, Retford

My Dog Joey

My dog Joey loves to play,
but not on a bad hair day.

He rolls about all day long,
but when he comes in there's a big pong.

My dog Joey loves to play,
but not on a bad hair day.

You'd think that he was a cat,
because he spends all day chasing the cat.

My dog Joey loves to play,
but not on a bad hair day.

Sam Johnson (9)
Ranskill Primary School, Retford

School

I go to a school which is very small,
We eat our sinners in the hall.
I like to play with my friends
And wish that playtime didn't end.
We have to learn a lot of things,
To read and write, act and sing.
We have lots of fun in our school
And our teachers are really cool.

Daniel Brownson (8)
Ranskill Primary School, Retford

My Brother

My brother is always in bother.
In the morning he tries to get into my bed,
But I pretend I am dead.

When I get breakfast
He always says what I say.
My brother is always in bother.

My brother is always in bother,
He always says no!
When I say yes.
My brother is always in bother.

My brother is so cute now he is 7,
He is never in bother.

Hannah Richardson (9)
Ranskill Primary School, Retford

The Woods In The Winter

The woods in the winter are usually white,
The crisp snow lands softly on the floor.
Crystal lakes glisten so bright,
While I walk through the woods in the winter.

The woods in the winter are usually white,
No leaves above to stop the sunlight,
Weak sunbeams shimmer through the branches,
While I walk through the woods in the winter.

The woods in the winter are too cold for me,
I'd rather be home by the fire,
So my footsteps follow the animal tracks home,
When I walk through the woods in the winter.

Jill Fleming (8)
Ranskill Primary School, Retford

School

S is for safe, SATs, swimming and school dinners
C is for concentration, computers and for completing work
H is for happiness, homework, holidays and healthy eating
O is for obedience, oranges and outside play
O is for OK teachers
L is for liking others, learning and loving being a community.

Kesson Wyld (8)
Ranskill Primary School, Retford

Four Seasons

Summer is warm
Summer is fun
There's always something good to be done
Hot sun, warm breeze
Always making so many sneeze
Paddling pools and water fights
The problem is mosquitoes bite.

Autumn rain and wind that makes leaves fall
I don't like this season at all
Trees bare and dusky light
Would give any brave person a fright.

Winter cold but never any snow
Christmas isn't that long to go
Cold winds, icy showers,
Come on spring
Let's see the flowers grow.

Small shrubs from the ground
In a couple of weeks the flowers will be found
Buds on trees
And buzzing bees
Get ready for sun
And warm summer fun.

Ryan Alder (9)
Ranskill Primary School, Retford

My Friend Amanda

My friend Amanda is like a panda,
She likes black and white,
She thinks she's so bright.
She tries to climb trees
But keeps getting stung by bees,
She stays out late at night
To try to fly a kite.
Then she comes in for bed
But runs and bumps her head,
That's my friend Amanda
Who's like a panda.

Caitlin Bennett (8)
Ranskill Primary School, Retford

My Brother

My brother looks like a big bright sun,
My brother feels like a big fluffy kitten,
My brother smells like perfume,
My brother tastes like a bunch of sweets.
My brother sounds like a piece of soft music,
My brother reminds me of sweet-smelling roses.

Sophie Windsor (8)
Rollesby First School & Nursery, Rollesby

My Family

My family looks like golden hearts,
My family feels like the softest things ever,
My family smells like flowers,
My family tastes like raspberries and strawberries,
My family sounds like happiness and laughing,
My family reminds me of happy things
That we have done with each other.

Loretta Askew (8)
Rollesby First School & Nursery, Rollesby

Happiness

Happiness looks like the bright sun,
Happiness feels like soft cotton wool.
Happiness smells like purple perfume,
Happiness tastes like lovely chocolate.
Happiness sounds like gentle, sweet music,
Happiness reminds me of lovely roses.
Happiness is great!

Maria Jacobs (7)
Rollesby First School & Nursery, Rollesby

Getting Up

Getting up looks like going to school,
Getting up feels like eating snails,
Getting up smells like lots of mud,
Getting up tastes like frogs,
Getting up sounds like thousands of children screaming,
Getting up reminds me of a rainy day.

Annabel Thain (7)
Rollesby First School & Nursery, Rollesby

Dinosaurs And Animals

Horses are quite fast.
Ponies are, but not as quick.
You can ride them both.
Lions are hunters,
And they live in groups called prides.
They will eat people.
Spiders crawl up pipes,
Spiders will crawl through gutters,
They go everywhere.
Raptors are vicious,
And they are small meat-eaters,
Raptors are quite fast.

Millie Hewkin (8)
Rollesby First School & Nursery, Rollesby

Happiness

Happiness looks like a bursting balloon,
Happiness feels like a woolly sheep,
Happiness smells like happy sun,
Happiness tastes like a lollipop,
Happiness sounds like someone,
Happiness reminds me of you.

Jasmine Williams (7)
Rollesby First School & Nursery, Rollesby

War

We declare war, war, war,
Even though we break the law, law, law.
The sound of firing guns, guns, guns,
To make people run, run, run.
Firing guns go bang, bang, bang,
In the castles you can get hanged, hanged, hanged.
Lots of people have shields, shields, shields,
And most of the people squeal, squeal, squeal.
Round the world there's war, war, war,
Lots of people break the law, law, law.
Most people fight for land, land, land,
Using weapons in their hands, hands, hands.

Anthony Abel (7)
Rollesby First School & Nursery, Rollesby

My Cat

My cat looks like the sun
My cat feels like a ball
My cat smells like flowers
My cat tastes like a sweet
My cat sounds like a miaow
My cat reminds me of happiness.

Alice Austin (8)
Rollesby First School & Nursery, Rollesby

I Wonder

I wonder what it would be like to have the world's sweetest bun,
I wonder what it would be like to have a Nintendo Wii must be
so much fun.

I wonder what would happen to you if you felt so much fear,
I wonder what it would be like to be a poet like Edward Lear.

It must be fun being in the world's best football team,
It must be like that for everyone, you would beam.

I wonder what is would be like to be the happiest person on Earth,
I wonder how terrible it would be to be sad from birth.

There are lots of things to wonder, like sad things and cool things,
Sometimes you might even wonder what it would be like to have no
feet, just wings.

David Kyei-Mensah (9)
St Thomas More Catholic Primary School, Leicester

Anger

I'm so annoyed with this poem
That I'm writing right now,
There's no shape,
No colour and definitely no confidence.

This poem I don't want around me anymore,
It's stupid,
Self-centred and always a show-off.

This poem I'm starting to hate right now
Because it doesn't show how I feel
About my own points.

This poem is . . .
War!

Isabella Oreffo (9)
St Thomas More Catholic Primary School, Leicester

Sadness

When my great grandma died,
It wasn't the same,
No more beautiful voice,
No, it's gone.

No more wide smile,
No more bulging blue eyes,
No more bedtime stories,
No, it's all gone.

It's not the same anymore,
All we've got are photos,
Just memories, that's all,
It's just not the same anymore.

Edward Ellis (9)
St Thomas More Catholic Primary School, Leicester

Meg The Dog

There was a dog called Meg,
Who begged, who begged, who begged.
But one day something happened,
Meg got very sick, I cried I cried, I cried.
But because she was in so much pain,
She got put down, I got a flower frame,
I got a picture of Meg, I put it in,
I'll said I'll never forget you again.

Katy Cooper (10)
St Thomas More Catholic Primary School, Leicester

I Love Polar Bears

Furry and white,
Cuddly and bright,
Polar bears come out at night.
Hunting for fish in an icy hole,
It's snowy and cold at the North Pole.
They're big, cute and funny,
What a shame they don't like honey!

Demi Boyce (9)
St Thomas More Catholic Primary School, Leicester

Why Emotions

Why does it have to be about emotions?
This poem I've got to write,
It's so annoying!

Why do I have to have ideas about everything else?
I'm *so* bored,
I'm *so* tired.

I want to be plunged into darkness,
I want to go to sleep,
To have something worthwhile to do.

But no, I've got write a poem about
Stupid, dumb, annoying, boring *emotions!*

Clare Ruane (9)
St Thomas More Catholic Primary School, Leicester

The Garden

As I cross the garden,
A wonderful feeling floods me,
A mixture of excitement and happiness,
All my worries forgotten.

But when I walk away from that magical place,
My heart aches with an empty sadness that won't go away.

I desperately try hard to make this pain go,
But it is only weakened by the power of the garden.
I spend as much time in it as I can,
Lying with the colourful scented flowers in perfect harmony.

I try hard, but I know I am not wanted in their house,
I pack up a tent and leave in the middle of the night.
I go to the garden and sleep peacefully among the plants and animals.

As time goes on the garden grows wildly, and so do I,
My hair is long and tangled and my clothes are dirty,
But that way I feel part of the slowly ageing garden.

Daisy Connolly (10)
St Thomas More Catholic Primary School, Leicester

Bullied

I sit in the playground,
Just me alone,
All my friends have left me.
Bullied, only for being a different skin tone.

Why they do it?
I just don't know,
But it makes me feel bad.
Bad, sad and low.

I run, I hide,
But nothing works.
For I always get bullied.
Just one thing that lurks.

What can I do?
What can I do?
There's nothing simple,
Yet I cannot sue.

There's only one thing I can do . . .
Begins with 't',
Ends with 'l',
That means I have to *tell.*

Imogen Howell (9)
St Thomas More Catholic Primary School, Leicester

A Snowy Day

I walked in the snow
With my friend called Mo
Our toes turned numb
And so did our thumbs.

We made a snowman
And a snow woman
He had a big nose
She had a rose.

We laid in the snow
We were very wet but we didn't know
A pond had frozen over
Which we skated on
But we fell on our bums.

By the end of the day
We were freezing
We shivered all the way home
I walked in the snow
And when I got home
I had a cup of cocoa.

Isabella Ambrico (10)
St Thomas More Catholic Primary School, Leicester

I Miss The Beautiful Girl

(Epitaph)

I miss her beautiful red lips,
That spoke words that did not harm.

Her skin was but a plain white,
But yet it was a beauty.

Her voice was as clear as a glint of sun
On the water in the lake.

But still I miss her most terribly,
When the sun is sinking
And the moon is rising, I mourn till the end.

Her style was the greatest, day and night,
And still her scent is hanging in the moonlit air.

I will never forget the gorgeous Belle White,
My best friend, the queen of beauty and love.
Who was kind, helpful and loving,
Who was and is still in my heart,
Forever, till my soul is dead.

Eleanor Pierson (10)
St Thomas More Catholic Primary School, Leicester

Anger

Anger is one of those horrible things,
I hate to use that horrible thing.
It's one of those things I hate to use,
I hate to use that horrible thing called anger.

Anger is my least favourite thing,
The thing I hate most is anger.
Whenever I use that horrible thing,
I always will regret it.

Anger is the thing I hate,
The thing I hate most is anger.
Whenever I use that horrible thing,
There's trouble round the corner.

Daniel O'Dwyer (9)
St Thomas More Catholic Primary School, Leicester

I Wonder What Is Out There

I listen to the silence,
When I am in my bed,
With darkness all around me,
Covers up to my head.

I wonder what is out there,
When it's dark at night,
With nothing to see by,
With not a single light.

But I am not afraid,
When I'm in my bed,
The strange things I imagine
Are only in my head.

James McErlean (10)
St Thomas More Catholic Primary School, Leicester

All Bullies Fail

They are the bullies
They are going to fail
I have manners
I will never fight

I just stand and watch them
I have manners

They call me names
In my heart it pains
They talk about me during class times
Well, maybe sometimes

Sometimes you have to say,
'The bullies have failed
And are never coming back again'

Let's celebrate for me
Hip hip for glee
That the bullies have failed just this time.

Lisa Konomoore (8)
St Thomas More Catholic Primary School, Leicester

Anger

One minute I'm happy
The next I'm sad
When I feel anger
It can be quite bad.

When things annoy me
I start seeing red
And then, before I know it
Nasty things I've said.

I feel like exploding
It has to come out
When it reaches its limit
I stamp, scream and shout.

When it's all over
And I've calmed down
I feel sorry
For all the chaos around.

Joe Muddimer (8)
St Thomas More Catholic Primary School, Leicester

Alone

I am alone
In the dark shadows
Trembling with fear
In the cold, cold street
I sit!

I am scared
I can't take it any longer
I think I'll go mad
In the cold, cold street
I sit!

I am afraid
The sun is not shining on me
All afraid
In the cold, cold street
I sit!

I've got rats nibbling at my feet
I don't know what to do
All alone
In the cold, cold street
I sit!

Ameerah Dawood (9)
St Thomas More Catholic Primary School, Leicester

Happy, Sad, Good, Bad

Sometimes I am happy,
Sometimes I am sad.

Sometimes I am good,
Sometimes I am bad.

When I am good it makes me feel happy,
When I am bad it makes me feel sad.

It's best for me to be good and happy,
Rather than be bad and sad.

Shannon Sheffield (8)
St Thomas More Catholic Primary School, Leicester

Happiness

Happiness, happiness, lots of things make it
Happiness, happiness! Happiness is a lot of things
Happiness, happiness feels good inside
Happiness, happiness is when something nice happens
Happiness, happiness is like a joke, just lasts for longer
Happiness, happiness might be a teddy bear
Happiness, happiness is when you're with the people you love
Happiness, happiness is when you're feeling fine
Happiness, happiness is fuzzy inside
Happiness, happiness is like snow, there for a moment then it's gone.

Kobe Whiteman (9)
St Thomas More Catholic Primary School, Leicester

What Makes Me Happy

H appiness is sunshine tickling my face.
A special time or moment, perhaps a special place.
P izza and some garlic bread, I'm always happy when I'm fed.
P laying games in the sand, music played by a band.
I ce creams I love on a summer's day, it always chases
my blues away.
N ight-time is when I am feeling dozy, tucked up in my bed all cosy.
E ating my mum's Sunday roast is the dinner I like most.
S iobhan is my friend and when we play I always have a happy day.
S inging in the choir makes my happiness even higher.

Niamh McErlean (8)
St Thomas More Catholic Primary School, Leicester

Laughter

Laughter is a nice sound, it spreads joy all around.
It does not matter if you're young or old,
Laughter will spread to your soul.
Whenever we are angry, laughter is the one.
Whenever we are sad, laughter is the one.
Whenever we are lonely, laughter is the one.
Laughter is the one.

Rose Leather (8)
St Thomas More Catholic Primary School, Leicester

Anger

Anger is like a hot volcano.
It can be an ice-cold stare.
You can feel burning inside you.
When you release it you can give them a scare.

Anger is like a big, big bang,
That can be heard far away in space,
An explosion, no collision,
And then things fall back into place.

Max Lewis-Clarke (9)
St Thomas More Catholic Primary School, Leicester

I Feel . . .

I feel . . .
A newborn puppy licking my nose,
A roller coaster ride going up and down,
Like having a midnight feast under the covers,
Like I'm gliding on ice,
Like opening a surprise present from someone special,
Popcorn popping in my belly,
The sea spraying on my face,
Sparkling fireworks in the sky,
Waves chasing me up the beach,
Like whizzing down a hill on my bike,
I feel . . . *ecstatic!*

Molly O'Halloran (10)
St Thomas More Catholic Primary School, Leicester

When I Play Table Tennis

I play quick,
I play slow,
I play high,
I play low.

I am happy,
I am sad,
I am good,
I am bad.

I play chop,
I play top!

Tobit Dehnen (9)
St Thomas More Catholic Primary School, Leicester

How Hill

When I was at How Hill
I saw the bright, bright house,
The tall windmill and a boat
And I could see a lot of woodpigeons
Flying overhead.

I could touch everything,
I could touch squishy things
Which were yucky.

I could smell some mole poo
And it smelt good!
I also smelt the lovely air.

I could hear the wonderful wind
Rustling amongst the trees
And the children laughing
And having fun.

I could taste the good cooking
In the kitchen
And the taste of the lovely place.

Harris Tzokas (7)
The Fairway First School, Norwich

How Hill Poem

At How Hill I saw a green boat
floating, floating all around
and a flock of beautiful swans.

I could hear people laughing,
I could hear the wind whistling
in the air.

I could smell food cooking
and the smell of the mud.

I could taste the chocolate cake
on the first night.

I could touch the silkiness
of the sleeping bag.

Jonathan Reynolds (7)
The Fairway First School, Norwich

How Hill Poem

At How Hill I could see a cute wood mouse
and a big, tall house.

At How Hill I could hear the wind blowing through the trees,
but sadly not the bumblebee.

At How Hill I could smell my chocolate bar melting
before I did my weaving.

At How Hill I could touch my bedroom bed,
that was luckily not wet.

At How Hill I could taste my Polo mints,
so these are my How Hill senses.

Alice Walker (7)
The Fairway First School, Norwich

Life At How Hill

I saw a boat and I saw lots of trees.
I saw leaves and voles and a wood mouse.

I heard a mallard in the river,
I heard the pitter-patter of the rain,
Shauna shouted when the wind blew.

I tasted the food,
I tasted the wind and the air.

I smelled the mud and the food,
I smelled the people and the air.

I felt the beds, the sleeping bags, the floor,
I felt the table and the chairs.

Fin Smith (8)
The Fairway First School, Norwich

My How Hill

At How Hill I could see bare trees
I could see the holly tree
I could see the inside of How Hill

I could hear the children talking
I could hear the children whistling
I could hear the birds singing

I could smell buns
I could smell chips
I could smell fresh air

I could taste chips
I could taste a sandwich
I could taste a bun

I could touch a vole
I could touch a water scorpion
I could touch a back swimmer.

Mia Morgan (7)
The Fairway First School, Norwich

The Swooping Poem

When I was walking in the woods,
I saw a tree waving in the wind.
It was really big.
It felt wet, it felt rough.
My hands were prickly because of the horrible roughness.

When I got into the boat it was really, really bumpy.
My hands were freezing,
And the wood on the boat was really soft.
The weed was waving in the wind, like I've never seen before.

I heard the air and birds swooping everywhere.
I heard the air in my ears, it felt very weird.
The swooping was really windy,
It's really hard, it swoops everywhere,
I really enjoyed it,
Birds flying everywhere.

I loved the smell of mud,
Air everywhere, it smelled squidgy,
It smelled gooey,
I loved the air and the mud everywhere.

Milo Butler (8)
The Fairway First School, Norwich

Life At How Hill

At How Hill I could see a boat
swirling near the edge of the river
near the land of marshes.

I could hear the birds tweeting
right in the morning, just quietly.

I could smell the mud
and the lovely food.

I could touch the air
floating in the sky.

I could taste the rain
dripping from the sky
just as the sun appeared.

Jaideep Chopra (7)
The Fairway First School, Norwich

My Very Funny Poem About How Hill

I caught sight of a mallard taking flight
When I was at How Hill House
I caught sight of a mouse
I could see a lovcly old tree
I could also see a vole.

I could taste the sausages and chips
I could taste my toast
I could taste the air and rain
I could taste the peas.

I could hear the squeak of a mouse
I could hear the crunch of a fish
I could hear the snuffle of a vole
I could hear the whirl of the windmill.

I could smell the chips
I could smell the yucky mud, really, really gross
I could smell the lovely meals.

I could feel the sticky, icky, yucky mud
Painted on my cheeks
I could feel the lumpy bark
Really, really hard.

Alex Wong (8)
The Fairway First School, Norwich

Life At How Hill

At How Hill I saw
lots and lots of fallen trees
that had come down straight.
In the dyke we caught a
swirling alder fly nymph.

At How Hill I tasted
my fruit and sandwiches.
When I was walking through
the mud I thought I was eating it,
I also thought I was drinking a thick drink.

At How Hill I heard a
bird that was squawking louder
than thunder in the dark grey sky.
It turned grey, it turned blue,
what was it going to do?

At How Hill I touched a log
and underneath there was
a tiny, weeny snail
slithering on some leaves.
I also touched my food,
my yummy, yummy food.

At How Hill I smelt the mud,
the yucky, yucky mud.
Squelching on my green wellie boots.
It was not very nice.
I also smelt the brand new gifts.

Charlie Grisley (8)
The Fairway First School, Norwich

Lovely How Hill

At How Hill I saw a beautiful, tiny snail, hiding under a log.
I saw a fallen tree in the squidgy, slimy mud.
At How Hill I could taste my lovely food.
But most of all I could taste my lovely sandwiches.
I felt like tasting the mud.

At How Hill I could touch the tall, thin trees.
I touched the short logs and a tiny snail.

At How Hill I could hear the birds singing in the sky,
I could hear the electric pump.

At How Hill I could smell the squidgy, slimy mud.
I could smell the lovely tasty food.

Eamon Hatoum (8)
The Fairway First School, Norwich

At How Hill

At How Hill I could see
The dyke as dirty as dirty can be!
In the dyke I saw some fleas.
The fleas were as tiny and teeny-weeny
and as squirmy and squiggly as fleas could be.

At How Hill I could taste
The lovely taste of breakfast,
And lunch and tea!
Er . . . sorry, but I didn't taste a flea!

At How Hill I could hear
The wind, the rain and the river.
The river was quite calm,
But I could still hear it anyway.

At How Hill I could smell
The smell of fresh fallen rain
And I could smell
The beautiful smell of meals being cooked.

At How Hill I could touch
The smooth, rough, bumpy
Barks of different trees
Swaying in the breeze.

Irene Ashworth (7)
The Fairway First School, Norwich

My How Hill Senses

At How Hill I could see
a wood mouse and a vole or two,
and see the big garden
and a bird swooping low.

At How Hill I could hear
children shouting, birds singing,
the fireplace whistling,
ducks quacking, people writing.

At How Hill I could smell the mud
and the lovely chips
and the fish fingers cooking.

At How Hill I could taste
yummy, yummy chips,
sausages, chocolate cake,
yummy, yummy fish fingers.

At How Hill I could touch
the big round tree
and the tiny acorn
and the thousands of dead leaves.

Alex Law (7)
The Fairway First School, Norwich

How Hill Nature

At How Hill I could see
A marsh harrier from the boat
And it was rare,
It was flying around some trees.

At How Hill I could smell
The fresh air,
It smelt good but the wind was howling.

At How Hill I could hear
The birds twittering in a tree.
I could also hear the raindrops, dripping onto the ground.

At How Hill I could taste
A raindrop, it tasted like water.

At How Hill I could touch
My wellie boots,
They felt a little bit rough.

Billy Breame (7)
The Fairway First School, Norwich

At How Hill

At How Hill I saw a big pond.
I could hear the trees waving.
I could smell the mud.
I could touch the trees.
I could taste my sandwich.

Haroon Said (7)
The Fairway First School, Norwich

Senses Around Yourself

At How Hill I could see
the wonderful green grass,
you could see the reeds dancing around
like a beautiful river floating by.

You could hear the birds chirping around,
looking for food on the long bright road,
going side by side.
Going down the hill, everywhere.

Did I go down the hill in the dark, spooky night?
Did I hear an owl flying away?
What did I hear every day?

I smelt the green, fresh grass,
you could smell the squelchy mud.
It's horrible to smell,
with the raindrops making a splashy sound,
it's mostly what I could smell.

You might taste the air
when you run really fast,
you could taste the food,
wanting more right away,
but if I was myself I would want
chocolate mustard with cake.

I could touch my shoes,
I could touch myself,
I could touch everything I liked,
even the air.

Shreya Arya (7)
The Fairway First School, Norwich

How Hill Poem

At How Hill I was in the boat
on the deep, blue water in the breeze.
I saw a marsh harrier swooping everywhere.

At How Hill the mud was all gooey
I touched it with my hands
it was slopping everywhere.

At How Hill I could taste
the chocolate spread sandwiches
running down my throat.

At How Hill I could smell the gooey mud.

Josh Bunn (7)
The Fairway First School, Norwich

At How Hill

At How Hill I saw some ducks
I heard birds tweeting
I tasted my ham sandwich
I touched the trees
I smelt the air.

Chloe Cox (8)
The Fairway First School, Norwich

Lovely How Hill

In the river I saw an insect
it was small and brown
and it was pointy and long.

I thought I heard a woodpecker.

I felt the trees,
some were wet and soggy,
some were rough, some were smooth.

I knelt down in the wet and soggy, squishy mud.

When I was running
I put my hands up in the air
and I felt the breeze.

I touched my butter and ham sandwiches
I took a bite and they were delicious.

When I went dyke dipping
the stick was wet and soft.

When I got back to school
my shoes were wet and soggy
and my socks were absolutely soaking wet!

Linton Garrod (8)
The Fairway First School, Norwich

How Hill Country

At How Hill I could see trees and weeds right in the ditch.
Mud here, mud there, mud everywhere.

I could taste the chips, the sausages and the jacket potato.

I could smell the stinky mud
And the lovely food cooking in the kitchen.

I could hear the wind blowing,
The trees shaking and the dyke splashing.

I could touch the food going into my mouth.
I could feel the rain coming from the sky.

Caleb Coxhead (8)
The Fairway First School, Norwich

Senses At How Hill

At How Hill I could see a big fat tree.

At How Hill I could hear a woodpecker
and the mud squelching.

At How Hill I could taste
the yummy fish fingers.

At How Hill I could smell the air.

At How Hill I wished I could touch the voles.

Louis Hall (7)
The Fairway First School, Norwich

Senses At How Hill

At How Hill I could see my friends
the trees and the brown leaves.

At How Hill I could smell the food
being cooked in the kitchen.

At how hill I could hear the wind
and the whistling in the air.

At How Hill I could taste
my lovely sandwich.

At How Hill I could touch
my two friends hands.

Sophie Bloomfield (7)
The Fairway First School, Norwich

My World At How Hill

At How Hill I saw the boats sliding
by on the river and the birds flying by in the sky
and the trees swishing to and fro.

I heard the mud squelching on the grass and leaves
and I heard the wind swooping in the sky.

I smell the lovely fresh air in the sky
and the lovely yummy food cooking in the kitchen.

I taste the yummy sandwiches in my tummy that I ate for lunch
and I taste the air swishing in my mouth when I speak.

I can touch the sloppy mud in my cold hand
and the soft gentle water swaying along.

Olivia Finch (7)
The Fairway First School, Norwich

Running Wild

I dream of running wild
through the open fields
in the woods between the trees,
among the flowers and the grass.
I dream of running wild.

I dream of running wild
in the heat of the sun,
in the cold of the snow,
in the bitterness of the wind and rain.
I dream of running wild.

I dream of running wild
with the spring air going through my hair,
the cold winter snow hitting my cheeks,
the summer sun blazing down.
I dream of running wild.

I dream of running wild
as I'm sleeping in my bed,
it's all going through my head,
no one to stop me,
as I dream of running wild.

Abbie Cochrane (10)
Waulud Primary School, Luton

A Beggar's Request

Do you have 50p to spare for me?
I need something to drink or eat
As I am skin and bones with no meat,
So please . . .
Do you have 50p to spare for me?

Do you have 50p to spare for me?
I promise you I'll spend it well,
This you know for no lies I tell,
So please . . .
Do you have 50p to spare for me?

Do you have 50p to spare for me?
Cheers, thank you,
Bless you, good day,
I'm sure it will help me on my way,
Thanks for the 50p you've spared for me!

Billie Hardiman (11)
Waulud Primary School, Luton

Revenge

I think of the wild cat, her smug grin.
My only cause is that sinful beast.
This torture I'm going through has to stop.
I'm surely barking mad.
She has made me become outraged,
But she has also made me guilty.
Oh, poor Parsnip and Squill, it is too late now.
Wild cats are such wretched creatures,
They create misery and pain,
Much worse than their deafening screech.
I know what I'll do,
I'll run, run for the hill.
The unclipped bracken claws at me as vicious as the wild cat.
I tear through the hedges that were my friends,
But now keep me from revenge.
My padded feet feel like little Alice's soft feet on this rough ground.
Spring . . . *Thud! Snap!*
My leg is wounded.

This wretched leg is nearly as bad
As carrying pups in your aching belly.
Now as I run onwards I see blurred visions of the village below,
My home, my life, I would have to leave.
The wild cat's disgusting stench is still under my nose.
I hear her kittens mewing from above.
I scamper up and howl into the night sky.
Unfortunately, now I return home to my one remaining pup.

Iaomie Malik (10)
Wellow House School, Newark

Poor Squill, Poor Parsnip

She broke my heart,
I will kill her,
I'll tear her apart,
no fear.

I must head for the forest,
with my precious pup,
before the mist,
blocks my way.

What's this I see?
Is it a ditch?
Thorns are pulling at me,
trip, clatter, thump, fall: silence

I'm weak and sad and full of hatred
towards a cat who might as well have plunged
a dagger through my heart.

I see the depressing, gloomy rubble of the banks of the ditch.
I hear poor, poor Hea Bane whimpering like a lost ghost
because of the cold.
I can feel my darling pup snuggling up beside me
to block out the howling of the cold, icy wind,
I smell the bitter smell of defeat and failure.

I have failed as a companion,
I have failed as a pet,
but most importantly I have failed as a mother.
Poor Squill.
Poor Parsnip.

Mary McQuilkin (11)
Wellow House School, Newark

Revenge

I felt cold, shivering and empty inside.
Sadness crept over me, like a cloud full of rain
but there was no rain, just tears, a thunderstorm of tears.
My pups had gone, I was only away for a few minutes,
but just like that, as part of my life, their future, was gone.

I galloped off towards the wood,
images of them being snatched away.
That awful cat, why did she do it?
How could she make anyone go through it?
I pounced over the fence just outside of the wood,
I landed and then slipped into a ditch,
I had to scramble up somehow, I had to get revenge.
I clambered, wincing and limped into the wood,
above my head her little demons lay,
I sat at the bottom, ready to pounce onto my prey.

Harriett Hawkins (11)
Wellow House School, Newark

Revenge

I'll kill it,
I'll rip its heart out
if it has one.
I'll snap its jaw
so it will never bite again.
I'll snap its nails
if that cat touches my pups.
It's horrible to think what's happened to them.
What's that smell?
It's her.
I stumble outside to pick up the scent,
run out through the garden
and over the fence.
I run and run
but the rain is lashing down on me.
Running up hills and sliding down banks,
but none of that matters to me.
I am just trying to keep up with the scent
before it is washed away.
I am as fast as light thundering through the forest,
with blurred images flashing by.
She has to be close.

Will Langley (11)
Wellow House School, Newark

How I Feel About The Beast Next Door

I feel terrible, everything's gone wrong,
I detest the wild cat for snatching my pups.
They could be dead.
I must set out to woods,
Where I will be safe.

I had to leave the house,
To hunt the wild cat,
To rip her apart.
I can hear the miaowing of her kittens in a tree.
I want them to know what their monstrous mother has done.
Then a wild scratch at the tree . . .
A howl.

Matt Badcock (11)
Wellow House School, Newark

The Storm

The storm is darting towards us like a peregrine falcon,
shooting like a bullet from a gun,
as deadly as the Grim Reaper,
sprinting like a cheetah.

Raging like a bull,
as powerful as a great white shark,
muscular as a blue whale,
mighty as the Apocalypse.

Noisy as a banshee,
loud as a lawnmower,
a din like an orca,
deafening as a threatening meteorite.

Damaging as an elephant,
devastating as a rhino,
destroys like a tiger shark,
splintering trees like a chainsaw.

Charles McQuilkin (10)
Wellow House School, Newark

The Great Storm

The storm rampages closer
like speeding asteroids and
leaping fireballs.

It's as powerful as rock
monsters that are 90 feet tall
jumping on all the buildings.

It sounds atrocious
like mumbling radios
and fuzzy TVs.

It damaged our field,
it left slushy, wet mud
on our fields and trees
on their last hinges.

Rive Malik (9)
Wellow House School, Newark

The Great Storm

It screams like a girl cries,
Blaring like a lion roaring.
I'm stuck inside and it's really boring.
It shrieks like a banshee.

It blows trampolines into smithereens,
It blows tree houses to obliteration.
The raging wind is like an almighty blizzard.
It's like tornadoes are in every square metre.

It's like a cheetah sprinting towards us,
With rockets strapped to his feet,
Like a bush fire setting alight,
As fast as a bouncing bomb.

Sad faces all around,
All the roots are out of the ground,
Scaffolding unable to stand up.
Today was the worst day.

William Cundy (9)
Wellow House School, Newark

The Horrible Storm

The storm was like a cheetah,
Getting closer and closer to its prey.
Rampaging like an elephant,
As fast as Muhammad Ali punching his opponent.
As fast as a gunshot.

As noisy as a screaming baby with a microphone,
As loud as a guitar and an amp on full blast,
As thunderous as an elephant.
As loud as billions of people screaming.

It kills trees like a chainsaw,
Wrecks trampolines like a rhinoceros,
As powerful as a polar bear,
Blowing the world up like an atomic bomb
Blowing up the galaxy.

Muscular and tough as rhinoceros hide,
As beefy as a lion,
Mighty as Marius Pujinowski.

Chloe Lidgett (10)
Wellow House School, Newark

The January 18th Storm

The storm was sprinting towards us
like a fierce, fighting fox on the run,
charging like lightning, springing light to light.
It was as powerful as a herd of bulls,
as loud as a roaring ram,
as mad as a moose.
It was tearing trampolines to pieces,
like an invisible chainsaw,
like a fire destroying everything.
It was like some scissors in its own control
cutting the wires loose,
and trees getting mad at each other,
snipping their own leaves off and pushing each other over.

Zoe Buckland (10)
Wellow House School, Newark

Striking Storm

Flying closer like the fastest eagle!
Diving like the most cunning vulture!
Swooping down on lorries like the strongest hawk!
Tearing up trees like the hungriest tiger!
Roaring like the angriest lion!
Burning out lights like water raging down a river!
Swishing through the trees like an invisible cancer!
Throwing away sticks like a mini tornado!
What its it? *The storm!*

Sam Lawrence (10)
Wellow House School, Newark

The Storm

Getting closer

It's getting nearer,
smashing down trees
like an angry man in a bulldozer.
Pushing away trampolines
like annoying flies,
blasting them away.

It's here

Crashing through the neighbourhood,
ripping tiles off roofs,
like a plough in a field
swiping away fences
like you're paying it to do it.

The noise

The noise is deafening,
screeching, screaming like a pierced balloon,
smashing, crashing, splintering trees,
it's terrible!

The aftermath

Walking around inspecting the damage,
branches off trees scattered all around,
the quiet, the eerie silence,
it's like a graveyard.

Jack Whitfield (10)
Wellow House School, Newark

The Great Storm Of Wellow

The storm is coming like a bush fire, but faster.
It's whirling and twirling like a tornado.

It is more powerful than an atom bomb,
It's so strong now, like a torpedo.

It sounds like a pack of wolves howling in the distance.
It's getting louder and louder, closer and closer.

The storm has left trees scattered,
Like people dead after a war.

Troy Booth (10)
Wellow House School, Newark

The Great Storm

Rushing towards us like an arrow.
Rapidly sprinting like a stormy sea.
Charging at us like a bull.
Racing at us like a cheetah.

Thrashing everything in its way like a piranha.
The wind was as boisterous as a rhino.
So strong that it picked up everything
In its way, like a tractor.

Screaming in your ear like a baby.
Like someone bashing cymbals for a whole day.
The bustling of leaves in you ear
Like a stampede rushing towards you.

Trashing trampolines to pieces like a bomb.
Wrecking tree houses like a troll with a sledgehammer.
Killing trees like an invisible axe.
Snapping electricity cables like a giant with some scissors.

Grace Brown (9)
Wellow House School, Newark

Wind On The Rampage

Approaching storm, howling wind,
Trees are creaking, cat's hairs on end;
Powerful blowing, blustering wind.
And with a crash, a very big smash, down comes a tree;
As if in slow motion, the black shape tumbles.
The wind is wailing, howling, shrieking,
Could have smashed the windowpane
And when darkness comes we cannot see,
'Cause we have no electricity!

Aiden O'Beirne (10)
Wellow House School, Newark

My Pet Poem

This is my rabbit, he's sharp as a thorn,
But this is my rabbit whose name is Storm.
My little rabbit, he's fast as the wind,
That why my love for him is very well pinned.
He has got a friend that's very old,
But stays in her nest so she never gets cold.
She's brown and white like potato mash,
But her real name is Flash.
That's the end of my love poem,
With Flash and Storm,
Still as sharp as a thorn.

Lizzie Lee (8)
Wellow House School, Newark

Untitled

I felt on the inside of me anger and sadness
that my pups had died,
so I went to find revenge on she who killed my pups;
and if she had babies I might just kill them
so she knows how it feels to have her babies killed.
I would kill her babies as well
so she can feel the pain as well.

I leapt out of the house
and sprinted following the smell,
as I ran through the wood
the branches were trying to stop me as I set out,
searching forever as I blinked,
I saw an image of my pups being eaten,
as I ran I got closer,
my veins started to tense up
and I felt the ten bullets that couldn't be stopped,
I could hear the laughing in my ears.

Ed Radley (11)
Wellow House School, Newark

Revenge

I am panicking so much,
Now my pups are gone.
I will destroy that cat's heart,
I'll assassinate my life,
Just to kill that cat's soul.
I enter the dark, wild wood,
I'll do anything to kill that cat.
As I enter the heart,
I pick up a smell.
I'm an unstoppable steamroller,
When my life is at risk,
I'll knock anything out of my path.
I smell the woodland,
I hear the rustling of leaves,
Under my paws as I scramble.
I try and try,
To defeat the brambles,
Climbing up my legs,
Pulling me down.
I'm all fired up,
I'm ready to pounce.
I hear the cat's kittens,
Up in a hollow tree.
I scale the tree,
Like a scampering squirrel.
I see the cat,
I look her in the eye.
First I'll kill her.
The her loveable kittens,
This is no battle,
This is a war.

Charles Broughton (11)
Wellow House School, Newark

Untitled

A tree tumbled like a pylon.
The rain flashed down like lightning.
The wind was like a hurricane.
The roar was like an air raid.
The wind was as loud as a plane.
The hail was as rapid as a waterfall.
The rain was as hard as an eagle snapping.
The roar was like the Earth was shaking.

Rosie Radley (10)
Wellow House School, Newark

Dentist

D entists pull your rotten teeth out, you'll scream.
E verybody is scared of the dentist and his drill.
N obody likes to go to the dentist but mums makes them.
T wo people I know like the dentist, I don't.
I absolutely hate the mean dentist.
S o I am at the dentist, hopefully he won't hurt me.
T he dentist gave me a lolly and now I like the dentist.

Aaron Homes (8)
Woods Loke Primary School, Oulton Broad

Give Up Slimming Mum

My Mum is short
and plump and pretty.
I wish she'd give up slimming,
So does Dad.
Her cooking's delicious,
you can't beat it,
but you really can
hardly bear to eat it
the way she sits,
with her eyes brimming,
watching you polish off,
the spuds and trimmings,
while she has nothing
herself,
but a small, thin,
dry, diet biscuit,
that's all.

Chloe Tiborez (8)
Woods Loke Primary School, Oulton Broad

My Pets I'll Never Forget

I have got a pet called Tinker,
sometimes he can be a little stinker,
he is a cheeky little hamster.
He runs up and down my mum and dad's legs,
he once even bit my brother on the neck,
I love my hamster very much.
We let him have a run in the lounge,
but my dad got cross when he ruined the carpet.
When I first bought my hamster
he had a twinkle in his eye,
I knew he was the one.
When I brought him home he was doing amazing tricks.
We clean him out every week,
and have a peek in his house,
he is a lovely pet.

Once I had a beautiful cat called Tibby,
she was a lovely cat.
We used to call her Tuna Tib,
because she loved tuna.
She was very kind.
She used to go to bed with me
and lay at the end of my bed.
She was the kindest cat in the world,
but one day she died,
I cried and cried and cried.
We buried her in the garden
and put her in with all her belongings.

I will never forget my lovely pets.

Isobelle Read (8)
Woods Loke Primary School, Oulton Broad

My Dolphin In America

My dolphin Katie loves fish
She lives in America but she'll always be mine.
She swims around like an octopus with all eight legs.
And pokes her nose up like a peg.

My dolphin had a friend once, called Ellie,
but sometimes Ellie could be wobbly like a jelly.
She always plays games with me
like hide-and-seek under water,
with all the other dolphins.

I also swam on her back with her,
she feels like leather.
I even kissed her and gave her a huge hug,
Before I came back to England.

Eleanor Sanders (9)
Woods Loke Primary School, Oulton Broad

I Had A Dream

I had a dream
that there was no more war.
I had a dream
that every football match was a draw.
I had a dream
that babies lived longer.
I had a dream
that I was stronger.
I had a dream
that I was a mouse.
I had a dream
that people didn't cry.
I had a dream
that people didn't die.

Frances Lear (9)
Woods Loke Primary School, Oulton Broad

Hero Time

His favourite colour is red,
he doesn't believe in the dead.

His favourite food is fish,
he always eats it on a dish.

He always helps his mates,
he really is ever so great.

He's really such a good mate,
he always waits for me at the gate.

But it turns out it was my dad all along.

Joshua Butcher (9)
Woods Loke Primary School, Oulton Broad

The Iron Man

On the top of the cliff,
The Iron Man stood,
As proud as the Prime Minister,
Tony Blair,
Over the sea,
The Iron Man would glare.
Then he was buried,
Under the farm,
Soon years went past,
Until the big crater appeared.
Everyone thought it was a charm,
But Hogarth knew,
The Iron Man had returned.

Charlie Church (9)
Woods Loke Primary School, Oulton Broad

My Feelings

I can be mad,
I can be sad.
I can be mean,
I can be lean.
I can be shy,
But I can't tell a lie.
I can play,
Sometimes all day.
I can be rough,
I can be tough.
But I like to be
Me!

I can cook,
I can read a book.
I can write,
I can fight.
I can stroke things,
I can poke things.
But I like to be,
Me!

Hannah Heath (9)
Woods Loke Primary School, Oulton Broad

Winter

Winter is cold,
But winter is fun,
We play with the snow
Until night comes.
You can hear the snow
Down in your feet,
Crushing and crackling,
Just like a sweet.

The robin looks lost,
But the birds all look cold,
The animals so frozen
They look like white frost.
They try to peck at the ground,
But there is nothing to be found.
What should we do?
They are starving for food!

Rebecca Thomas (8)
Woods Loke Primary School, Oulton Broad

Wildlife

Have you ever seen a tiger,
Pouncing on its prey?
Ever seen a dolphin
Swimming in the sea?
There's a lovely lot of animals
Waiting to be found,
Will you come and help me
Look around the land?

I have seen a cheetah
Looking for its prey.
I have seen a lion
Eating all his meat.
That a few of the animals
Waiting to be found.
Now I'll come and help you
Look around the land.

People crying,
Animals dying,
Things like dolphins
And squirrels too.
Help me out,
They need to survive,
Help the zoo,
I'm the keeper,
Help save the animals!

Bethany Paisley (8)
Woods Loke Primary School, Oulton Broad

Young Writers Information

We hope you have enjoyed reading this book - and that you will continue to enjoy it in the coming years.

If you like reading and writing poetry drop us a line, or give us a call, and we'll send you a free information pack.

Alternatively if you would like to order further copies of this book or any of our other titles, then please give us a call or log onto our website at www.youngwriters.co.uk

Young Writers Information
Remus House
Coltsfoot Drive
Peterborough
PE2 9JX

(01733) 890066